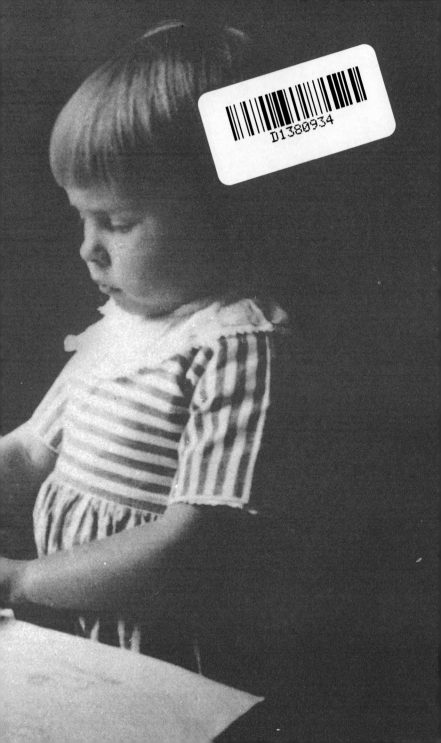

Sculptor's Daughter

Tove Jansson

Sort Of
BOOKS

Sculptor's Daughter

A CHILDHOOD MEMOIR

Tove Jansson

with an introduction by

Ali Smith

translated by

Kingsley Hart

Sculptor's Daughter © Tove Jansson 1968
First published (as *Bildhuggarens Dotter*) by Schildts Förlags Ab, Finland.
English translation © Schildts Förlags Ab, Finland 1969
All rights reserved

This English edition first published in 2013 by
Sort Of Books, PO Box 18678, London NW3 2FL.

Distributed by Profile Books
3a Exmouth House, Pine Stree, London EC1R 0JH.

10 9 8 7 6 5 4 3 2

No part of this book may be reproduced in any form without permission
from the publisher except for the quotation of brief passages in reviews.

Typeset in Goudy and Gill Sans to a design by Henry Iles.
Printed in the UK by Clays Ltd, St Ives plc.

Thanks to Sophia Jansson for her encouragement and advice, and to
Peter Dyer, Henry Iles and Susanne Hillen for design and proofreading.

192pp.
A catalogue record for this book is available from the British Library.

ISBN 978-1908745330
ePub ISBN 978-1908745347

Contents

Introduction
by Ali Smith

A SMALL CHILD IS DIGGING A HOLE in one of the walls of the city apartment she lives in with her parents. It's solitary work, but she's already 'got quite a long way … the wooden panelling went all right but then I had to use the marble hammer.' Luckily her father is a sculptor so she has the tools to hand; in fact the hole she's digging is in his studio wall.

She's making a 'secret tunnel' in a story called *The Dark*, because danger, when you're a child, 'lies in wait everywhere.' After you're born pretty much everything is dangerous, the child announces at the end of this story, which begins with a nightmarish landscape – a too-gothic church, foul jagged rubbish glinting everywhere, locked doors, a house with no windows – and goes on to transform an innocent visit to the ice rink into 'the worst thing of all', a vision of existentialism in which 'hundreds of shadowy figures skate round and round, all in the same direction, resolutely and pointlessly.'

The pile-up of terrifying images – not just dark ice and Scandinavian gloom, but snakes, monsters, a visit to the waxworks where 'you can see how easy it is to smash people to pieces ... crushed, torn in half or sawn into little bits' – becomes grist to the mill in a piece which turns into a children's game, funny and fast, moving at the speed of light and transforming danger into something exhilarating, the child ricocheting in near-euphoria between the joy and the fear of feeling anything at all.

But there's something else, something other than this game, at the heart of it. Her father isn't the only artist in the house, her mother is one, too; the child, descended from art, is hiding her escape tunnel behind a wall-hanging of a painting her mother made when she was young, of evening light in a wood, and when the child looks at this painting she knows that there's an even more intense state of feeling possible, something more powerful than self-torture and frenetic destruction, more powerful even than going into hiding.

> Everything except the sky has gone dark in a vague greyish brown but there are narrow red streaks that burn like fire. I love her picture. It goes deep into the wall, deeper than my hole ... it goes on endlessly and one never gets to the place where the sun is setting but the red gets more and more intense. I'm sure it's burning!

Art and life, light and dark, child's play and deadly seriousness, hilarity and despair, creativity and existential cataclysm, and all of these oppositions held simultaneously and brought to work together: this is Tove Jansson territory. More, *Sculptor's Daughter*, originally published in Finland as *Bildhuggarens Dotter* back in 1968, could be said to be closer to home for Tove Jansson than any of her other fictional works.

TOVE JANSSON WAS BORN in Helsinki in 1914 into an avowedly artistic family. Her father, Viktor Jansson, was a Finnish sculptor and her mother, Signe Hammarsten-Jansson, or Ham to her children, was Swedish, an illustrator, graphic designer and caricaturist, and a career woman who eventually designed Finnish postage stamps, watermarks and banknotes. For Ham, art was work and work was money, especially since there wasn't much sure money in sculpture. Tove, born in July 1914 on the eve of the First World War, was a professional artist and writer herself as early as her mid-teens.

She began the first of the series of books for children that would make her internationally famous, the books about the Finn Family Moomintroll, in the middle of yet another war, publishing it in 1945; the story goes that she wrote and drew *The Moomins and the Great Flood*, a work centred on innocence and naivety, consciously to dispel some of the foulness, darkness and depression of the Second World War years.

The Moomins and the Great Flood, only very recently published in English for the first time, is a book of darkness, mud and storms, where a mother and child, travelling to find both a home and the family's father, light their way with a tulip, find sun and hospitality and befriend many creatures on their journey. At one point they set sail using an armchair for a boat:

> 'Go carefully!' cried the small creature. He was sitting on the backrest and looking around, for it had occurred to him that they might find something valuable floating in the water after the flood. For example a casket full of jewels. Why not? He kept a sharp watch, and when he suddenly saw something gleaming in the water, he shouted loudly with excitement. 'Go that way,' he cried. 'There's something shining over there.'

It's only an old bottle, not treasure at all, but of course there's a message in it. One of Jansson's own repeated messages-in-a-bottle to us over the course of a lifetime of art and writing – seven decades of work (she died in 2001), for people of all ages – is that there'll always be treasure gleaming somewhere in what you salvage, and it'll probably be unexpected.

The phrase 'less is more' might have been coined specifically for an aesthetic practice like Jansson's. She was a consummate editor, a composer of prose so tightly disciplined that the end effect is somehow universal and cornucopic. In Jansson's work, smallness, and attention to the smallest detail, most often leads her reader to something more like epic in understanding; and matters and practices in art and in prose are always, for her, related to matters of living and surviving. As the child puts it in the story called *Flotsam and Jetsam* in *Sculptor's Daughter*, a story about all sorts of salvage and surprises as well as how to live communally and graciously in a wild and stormy world, 'one mustn't have a single unnecessary thing in a boat.'

SCULPTOR'S DAUGHTER WAS WRITTEN ten years after the death of Jansson's father, when her mother was 86 (Ham died in 1970). By now Jansson was working towards what would be the last, the darkest and the wintriest of the Moomin books, *Moominvalley in November*. 'I want to write something new,' she told her partner, the graphic artist, Tuulikki Pietilä, 'in fully adult mode yet about what is still a small world.' *Sculptor's Daughter* was the first of a dozen texts that Jansson would write specifically for adults rather than children, an important book in this transition for her, a threshold work; the next thirty years of her life would be devoted to fiction for adults.

Since the republication of her 1972 novel *The Summer Book* in the UK ten years ago, a steadily growing readership here has seen several of Tove's works (and there are many more to come, which is tremendously exciting) become available in English, often for the first time. Each of these discoveries or rediscoveries is itself a sort of surprise, a fresh illumination of the quiet brilliance of Jansson's aesthetic. Now, as we approach the centenary of her birth in 2014, *Sculptor's Daughter* is back in print here for the first time in over forty years. It is the revelation of a classic.

Though it is the most admittedly autobiographical of her books, Jansson, who 'fought shy of biographies,' all her life, would never herself have called it a memoir. Is it one? Strictly, no. But her

Tove Jansson's artwork for the original Swedish publication of
Bildhuggarens Dotter (Sculptor's Daughter), Schildts, 1968.

books are always more than one thing (the only strictness she's ever interested in as a writer is aesthetic, like the tightness of edit mentioned above) and, in the same way as her writing for children can be read with an adult philosophical eye, allowing, in books written primarily for children, the child and the adult to co-exist, *Sculptor's Daughter* is versatile. One of the things it goes out of its way to do is to return child consciousness and child logic to the adult state, complete with the wisdom of aftermath and experience. It might also be said to function as an aesthetic primer; it teaches its reader, both primally and with sophistication, about art and the uses of art, it is all about art's own versatility. Most of all, it is a calibrated work of art, of the imagination, in itself.

In it, a sculptor father who treats his studio and his work as sacrosanct (and expects everybody round him to) sculpts alongside an artist mother who works exceptionally hard, mostly for money ('like in town when drawing was done at night and made you so tired that you felt sick'). The child inherits both modes, the mother's disciplined practicality and the father's more ceremonial theatricality.

The collection examines art and competitiveness in a world where the worst insult is the word amateur. 'You're not a real artist!' the child shouts at a woman she's jealous of. 'You're nobody's surprise!' There's a lesson in how to focus: 'you can close your mind to things if something is important enough. It works very well. You make yourself very small, shut your eyes tight and say a big word over and over again until you're safe' (*The Stone*). There's a lesson in how art can protect: 'I captured this cruel thing on paper so that it couldn't get at me' (*The Dark*). There's a lesson in how to draw a forest, in *The Bays*, a story about our responsibility towards the landscapes we inhabit – a story in which child becomes landscape and landscape becomes child, time disappears and the telling of stories allows the imagination space and the space we inhabit its own wild imagination: 'That was a good story – Another one.'

Safety is a grave matter in *Sculptor's Daughter*, where the telling of stories is more than just an act of pleasure, it's a ritual connected with warmth, security and home. There are rules everywhere; part of the joy of the book is in the following of them but a large part is in the breaking of them, the acceptance of natural wildness: 'it was marvellous! The grass was under water, the sea was rising all the time, and the storm and the night made the whole landscape look quite different.'

One of the sources of power throughout is Jansson's effortless-seeming ventriloquism, her delivery of the child's voice, a device as clear as water, or perhaps as magnifying and altering (and as deceptive when it comes to true depth) as looking through clear water. Voice throughout *Sculptor's Daughter* is an amalgam of formal and informal, a fusion of innocence and irony in the parroting of the parents' practicality and theatricality; it inhabits both the past tense and the present in a multiconsciousness of both which is only the beginnings of its skilled implication. It is never sentimental. It can reveal in a throwaway comment – like 'women always forgot to shut doors after them,' or Females 'are asocial and wouldn't even obey orders during a war' – what's routinely said, what's acceptable and what's expected, as well as what's not being said, what can't be said and what's undercurrent in everything that's said.

Jansson's use of form is also deceptive, and masterfully subtle. The collection apes simplicity, looks at the outset to be a series of haphazardly organized childhood vignettes. On a closer look, each of its stories is a piece of discrete virtuoso; this is a book full of stories, each separately so good, so expertly judged that this would be more than enough; but best and quietest of all (and Jansson is a master of the quietness of form) each one is unexpectedly the source of what comes after it, each one blooms unforeseeably out of the one before. A word or phrase casually used in one will be the germ or seed for the next. It's almost invisible, as a formal device, only there if you really look. A mention of a grandmother hiding things under a skirt in *The Spinster Who Had An Idea* is followed by a full-blown, under-the-skirt story, *The Tulle Skirt*, where the child hides herself under one and looks out through it at the apartment as a dramatic new world. A throwaway moment in *The Tulle Skirt*, the image of an open window which happens to let a casual, pretty drift of snow fall on the apartment floor, gives way to *Snow*, a story where the child and her mother survive in a house under deep snow – a story about how stories connect us, and how a sharing of stories is the opposite of solitariness. The book is a masterpiece of this formal lightness of touch, and of an undercurrent connectivity. And, as the child knows, in art 'making a whole is very important. Some people just paint things and forget the whole' (*Parties*).

THERE ARE REAL PEOPLE here in these stories. Real things that happened to Tove Jansson and her family pass through them all: she really did sleep in a bunk high up on a shelf; her father really did have a pet monkey; her mother really did work that hard; and they really did spend summers on an island and winters in the city. Work colleagues and artist friends of her parents flit in quick-footed cameos through the text. Perhaps most delightfully of all it's interesting to know that the small drippy-nosed child called Poyu, who also loves to be tormented by fear in that story called *The Dark*, grew up in real life to become the Sibelius expert Erik Tawaststjerna.

'*Sculptor's Daughter* is indeed about my childhood,' Jansson wrote to Tordis Orjasaeter, who was compiling a sort-of biography (it was for teenagers, which is why Jansson agreed to let her) in 1983, 'but naturally a certain amount has been added.' Take the story that opens the collection. In *The Golden Calf*, Jansson wrote to Orjasaeter, 'everything really happened except the calf.' But as the title itself suggests, the calf – the invention by which means she departs from autobiographical truth – is the whole point.

The story makes its subject – authority – biblically clear from the start (and it's the opening of the book, too, which suggests that authority, and generation, will be important concepts in the collection):

> Grandfather was a clergyman and used to preach to the King. Once, before his children and his children's children and his children's children's children covered the face of the earth, Grandfather came to a long field which was surrounded by forests and hills so that it looked like Paradise.

Here in this place strung between the past and the future, God looks 'just like Grandfather', rather than the other way round, and fertility is a matter of such authority, since if Grandfather even deigns to point at a plant, 'it was blessed and grew until it groaned under its own weight.' It's a story of the groaning in the growing, then – both comic and real.

The child and her mother (there's no mention of a father in this opening story) have come to stay 'in the West Room, which also had white furniture and peaceful pictures but no sculpture'. So the first mention of sculpture in a book called *Sculptor's Daughter* is of its absence. This child of something absent, from somewhere else, finds herself helplessly placed in competition almost as soon as she exists, up against another grandchild who has the advantage of being pretty and having naturally curly hair. They go round in a holier-than-thou competitiveness, trying to get God's attention. 'We raised our voices in the wilderness and were continually disobedient because God so likes to forgive sinners.' When Karin, the other grandchild, gets ahead in the game, the child decides to do the worst, most blasphemous and pagan thing she can think of. 'It was then that I made the golden calf.' She makes her first sculpture, then she waits for God to be furious and 'show that he knew that I existed.' Her grandmother comes out, looks at the calf, decides the child has been playing a pretty game and calls the sculpture 'God's little lamb.' The child is disgusted, both with life and with herself.

In this very funny story about how we make, react to and disrupt authorities, the act of art becomes charged with power, then with failure. This is what the sculptor's daughter will be up against – the misjudgements and preconceptions, the misinterpretations, the age-old entrenched beliefs, traditions and authorities, the inevitable failures and competitions and the games you have to play – in the course of the childhood, the course of the book. The rights and wrongs, not just of art but of existence, are its real subject. 'What is right and what is wrong is a very sensitive matter,' as she says elsewhere in a collection whose title foregrounds the child's gender but whose stories never once refer to it, a collection in which there's a core of stories at the centre specifically about what it means, in this world, to be female. *Sculptor's Daughter* acts as an implicit (and sometimes quite explicit, unexpectedly blatant) critique. The child state, she reminds us, is refreshingly free from preconception – as well as a sponge for it, something that alarmingly absorbs it. From story to story we see the closedness of preconception and the child, unknowing, up against it.

Unknowing? 'I know. I know a lot that I don't talk about.' For instance, the war, especially the

Finnish Civil War of 1918, which arose out of the turmoil of the First World War, runs like a dark and near-unspoken undercurrent through these stories much as it did through the child Tove's early years of life; her father Viktor returned from the fighting, only thirty-two, a young but much darkened man, according to Boel Westin's biography of Tove Jansson.

So the story called *Parties*, ostensibly a charming and funny look at drunken social evenings, but really an analysis of art and hospitality as sources of reparation, has at the heart of it a violence and an unspeakable pain; and the opening story, *The Golden Calf*, is, in autobiographical terms, about real absence, the time Jansson and her mother spent in Sweden with her mother's parents when she was very small and her father was at war.

This biographically explains *Sculptor's Daughter*'s preoccupation with the dark and its preoccupation with authority, fear and salvage ('in the end we saved everything that could be saved'). But only artistry explains the confluence of darkness, illumination, kindness and understanding which results in a book full of images as unsettling, surreal, vivid and full of unexpected light as the one in the story called *The Iceberg*, where the child, on her summer island and fascinated by a small floating 'grotto' of an iceberg offshore, goes out with a light in the middle of the night with a plan to throw herself inside it and float away. At the last minute she loses her nerve and throws her father's torch instead. The ice lights up. But we're left with both images, the one which doesn't exist, conjured all the same, of a lost and frozen child, a child tucked inside an iceberg far out at sea, and this image which does, and which the child, annoyed at herself for not being brave enough to jump, consoles herself with:

> My iceberg shone steadily out there like a green beacon and the batteries would last until sunrise because they were always new when one had just moved to the country. Perhaps ... the torch would go on shining at the bottom of the sea after the iceberg had melted and turned into water.

From its foothold on the icy surface, *Sculptor's Daughter* lights these surprising depths. It demands an understanding of the importance, and the fragility, geologically and metaphysically, of our smallness. It asks us to be alive to the imagination when it comes to the world, the ways we live and the different ways we can live. It mends its own breakages with art and story; this reparation always involves the telling of a good story, and then, when that story's finished, another one. It is full of flung-open windows, thrown-open doors. At one point, at the end of the story called *The Stone*, a story about unexpected sources of wealth and about discovering a source of unexpected brightness in, of all things, stone, the child literally finds herself 'squeezed in', caught between 'double doors with coiled iron springs at the top which the caretaker had put there because women always forgot to shut the doors.' She's the wedge that forces them open and keeps them open.

It's a memoir of the child Tove Jansson. It's a book of superb stories. It's a connective master-piece, a literal and literary threshold-maker in itself, sharp to and dismissive of all the closed doors; a book whose small, huge work is the healing of the divisions between the child state and the adult state, and whose huge ambition and painstaking micro-work is the salvaging and the giving back to adulthood, in the dangerous dark times there will always be, of a child-sized truth about how things connect, how they mend and how they continue, one good story after another.

Publisher's note: *The stories in this book follow Tove Jansson's original edition of* Sculptor's Daughter, *published in Swedish in 1968. The images, taken from the Jansson family archive, were added to the Swedish edition in 2003; see 'A note on the photos' at the end of the book for descriptions. Thirteen of the stories were included in the Sort Of Books collection,* A Winter Book: Selected Stories.

Sculptor's
Daughter

Tove Jansson

The Golden Calf

GRANDFATHER WAS A CLERGYMAN and used to preach to the King. Once, before his children and his children's children and his children's children's children covered the face of the earth, Grandfather came to a long field which was surrounded by forests and hills so that it looked like Paradise. At one end it opened out into a bay for his descendants to bathe in.

Then Grandfather thought, here will I dwell and multiply, for verily this is the Land of Canaan.

Then Grandfather and Grandmother built a big two-storey house with a sloping roof and lots of rooms and steps and terraces and a huge veranda and placed plain wooden furniture everywhere inside and outside the house and when it was ready Grandfather began to plant things until the field became a Garden of Eden where he walked around in his big black beard. All he had to do was to point at a plant and it was blessed and grew until it groaned under its own weight.

The whole house was overgrown with honey-suckle and Virginia creeper and walls of small rambler roses grew round the veranda. Inside these walls Grandmother sat in a pale-grey silk dress and brought up her children. There were so many bees and bumble bees flying around her that it sounded like soft organ music, and in the daytime it was sunny and at night it rained and in the rock-garden there lived an angel who wasn't to be disturbed.

She was still there when Mummy and I went out to live in the West Room, which also had white furniture and peaceful pictures but no sculpture.

I was a grandchild. Karin was another grandchild but her hair curled naturally and she had very big eyes. We played The Children of Israel together in the field.

God lived on the hill above the rock-garden and there was a forbidden cart up there. At sunset he spread out like a mist over the house and the field. He could make himself quite small and creep in everywhere in order to see what one was doing and sometimes he was only a great big eye. Moreover he looked just like Grandfather.

We raised our voices in the wilderness and were continually disobedient because God so likes to forgive sinners. God forbade us to gather manna under the laburnum tree but we did all the same. Then he sent worms up from the earth to eat up the manna. But we went on being disobedient and we still raised our voices.

All the time we expected him to get so angry that he would show himself. The very idea was tremendous. We could think of nothing but God. We sacrificed to him, we gave him blueberries and crab apples and flowers and milk and sometimes we made a small burnt-offering. We sang for him and we prayed to him to give us a sign that he was interested in what we were doing.

One morning Karin said that the sign had come to her. He had sent a yellow bunting into her room and it had perched on the picture of Jesus Walking on the Waters and nodded its head three times.

Verily, verily I say unto you, Karin said, many are called but few are chosen.

She put on a white dress and went round all day with roses in her hair and sang hymns and carried on in a very affected way. She was more beautiful than ever and I hated her. My window had been open too. I had a picture of the Guardian Angel at the Abyss on my wall. I had burnt as many burnt-offerings and picked even more blueberries for him. And as for raising my voice in the wilderness I had been just as disobedient as she in order to get divine forgiveness.

At morning prayers on the veranda Karin looked as though Grandfather was preaching only to her. She nodded her head slowly with a thoughtful look on her face. She clasped her hands long before the Lord's Prayer. She sang with great emphasis and kept her eyes on the ceiling. After that business of the yellow bunting God belonged to her.

We didn't speak to each other and I stopped raising my voice in the wilderness and sacrificing and was so jealous that I felt sick.

One day Karin lined up all the cousins in the field, even the ones who couldn't talk yet, and held a Bible class for them.

It was then that I made the golden calf.

When Grandfather was young and was planting like mad he put a circle of spruce trees at the bottom of the field because he wanted a little arbour to have his afternoon tea in. The spruce trees grew and grew until they were huge and black and their branches got all tangled up with each other. It was quite dark inside the arbour and all the needles fell off and lay on the ground because they never got enough sunshine. Nobody wanted to have tea there any longer but preferred to sit under the laburnum or on the veranda.

I made my golden calf in the arbour because it was a pagan place and a circle is always a good setting for sculpture. It was very difficult to get the legs to stay upright but in the end they did and I nailed them to the plinth just to make sure. Sometimes I stood still, listening for the first rumble of the wrath of God. But so far he had said nothing. His great eye just looked right down into the arbour through the hole between the tops of the spruce trees. At last I had got him to show some interest.

The head of the calf turned out very well. I used tin cans and rags and bits of a muff and tied the lot together with string. If you stood a little way away and screwed up your eyes the calf really did shine like gold in the darkness, particularly round its nose.

I became more and more interested in it and began to think more and more about the calf and less and less about God. It was a very good golden calf. Finally I put a circle of stones round it and collected dry twigs for a burnt-offering.

Only when the burnt-offering was ready to light did I begin to feel afraid again and I stood completely still and listened.

God kept completely quiet. Perhaps he was waiting for me to take out the matches. He wanted to see if I really would do something so awful as to sacrifice to the golden calf and, even worse, dance in front of it afterwards. Then he would come down from his hill in a cloud of lightning and wrath and show that he knew that I existed. Then Karin could keep her old yellow bunting and her prayers and her blueberries!

I stood there and listened and listened and the silence grew and grew until it was overpowering. Everything was listening. It was late in the after-noon and the light coming through the trees made the branches look red. The golden calf looked at me and waited and my legs began to feel weak. I started to walk backwards, towards the gap between the trees, looking at the calf all the time, and as it became lighter and warmer I thought that I should have signed my name on the socle.

Grandmother was standing outside the arbour and she was wearing her lovely grey silk dress and her parting was as straight as an angel's.

What have you been playing at in there, she said, and walked straight past me. She stood in front of the golden calf and looked at it and smiled. She put her arm around me and absent-mindedly pressed me against the grey silk and said: look what you've made! A little lamb. God's little lamb!

Then she let go of me and walked slowly down the field.

I stayed where I was and my eyes began to smart and the bottom fell out of everything and God went back to his hill again and calmed down. She hadn't even noticed that it was a calf! A lamb! Good grief! It didn't look one little bit like a lamb, nowhere near it! I stared and stared at my calf. And what Grandmother had said seemed to have taken all the gold away from it and the legs were wrong and the head was wrong, everything about it was wrong and if it looked like anything at all perhaps it was a lamb. It wasn't any good. It wasn't sculpture at all.

I went to the junk room and sat there for a long time and thought. I found a sack. I put it on and then went out into the field and shuffled around in front of Karin on bended knee with my hair hanging over my eyes.

Whatever are you doing? Karin asked.

Then I answered: verily, verily I say unto you, I am a great sinner.

Really? said Karin. I could see that she was impressed.

Then everything was as usual again, and we lay under the laburnum tree and whispered together about God. Grandfather walked up and down making everything grow and the angel was still there in the rock-garden as if nothing had happened at all.

The Dark

BEHIND THE RUSSIAN CHURCH there is an abyss. The moss and the rubbish are slippery and jagged old tins glitter at the bottom. For hundreds of years they have piled up higher and higher against a long dark red house without windows. The red house crawls round the rock and it is very significant that it has no windows. Behind the house is the harbour, a silent harbour with no boats in it. The little wooden door in the rock below the church is always locked.

Hold your breath when you run past it, I told Poyu. Otherwise Putrefaction will come out and catch you.

Poyu always has a cold. He can play the piano and holds his hands in front of him as if he were afraid of being attacked or was apologising to someone. I always scare him and he follows me because he wants to be scared.

As soon as twilight comes, a great big creature creeps over the harbour. It has no face but has got

9

very distinct hands which cover one island after another as it creeps forward. When there are no more islands left it stretches its arm out over the water, a very long arm that trembles a little and begins to grope its way towards Skatudden. Its fingers reach the Russian Church and touch the rock – oh! Such a great big grey hand!

I know what it is that's the worst thing of all. It's the skating-rink. I have a six-sided skating badge sewn to my jumper. The key I use to tighten my skates is on a shoelace round my neck. When you go down onto the ice, the skating-rink looks like a little bracelet of light far out in the darkness. The harbour is an ocean of blue snow and loneliness and nasty fresh air.

Poyu doesn't skate because his ankles wobble, but I have to. Behind the rink lies the creeping creature and round the rink there is a ring of black water. The water breathes at the edge of the ice and moves gently, and sometimes it rises with a sigh and spreads out over the ice. When you are safely on the rink it isn't dangerous any more but you feel gloomy.

Hundreds of shadowy figures skate round and round, all in the same direction, resolutely and pointlessly, and two freezing old men sit playing in the middle under a tarpaulin. They are playing 'Ramona' and 'I go out of an evening but my old girl stays at home'. It is cold. Your nose runs and when you wipe it you get icicles on your mittens.

Your skates have to be fixed to your heels. There's a little hole of iron and it's always full of small stones. I pick them out with the key of my skates. And then there are the stiff straps to thread through their holes. And then I go round with the others in order to get some fresh air and because the skating badge is very expensive. But there's no one here to scare, everybody just skates faster, strange shadows making scrunching and squeaking noises as they pass.

The lamps sway to and fro in the wind. If they went out we should keep going round and round in the dark, and the music would play on and on and gradually the channel in the ice would get wider and wider, yawning and breathing more heavily, and the whole harbour would be black water with only an island of ice on which we would go round and round for ever and ever amen.

Ramona is as pretty as a picture and as pale as The Thunder Bride. Ramona is for adults only. I have seen The Thunder Bride at the waxworks. Daddy and I love the waxworks. She was struck by lightning just when she was going to get married. The lightning struck her myrtle wreath and came out through her feet. That's why she is barefoot, and you can see quite clearly lots of crooked blue lines on the soles of her feet where the lightning came out again.

At the waxworks you can see how easy it is to smash people to pieces. They can be crushed, torn in half or sawn into little bits. Nobody is safe and therefore it is terribly important to find a hiding-place in time.

I used to sing sad songs to Poyu. He put his hands over his ears but he listened all the same. Life is an isle of sorrow, you live today and die tomorrow! The skating-rink was the isle of sorrow. We drew it underneath the dining-room table. With a ruler Poyu drew every plank in the fence and the lamps all at the same distance from one another and his pencil was always too hard. I only drew black and with a 4B – the darkness on the ice, or the channel in the ice or a thousand murky figures on squeaking skates flying round in a circle. He didn't understand what I was drawing, so I took a red pencil and whispered: Marks of blood! Blood all over the ice! And Poyu screamed while I captured this cruel thing on paper so that it couldn't get at me.

One Sunday I taught Poyu how to escape from the snakes in their big carpet. All you have to do is walk along the light-coloured edges, on all the colours that are light. If you step on the dark colours next to them you are lost. There are such swarms of snakes there you just can't describe them, you have to imagine them. Everyone must imagine his own snakes because no one else's snakes can ever be as awful.

He balanced himself with tiny, tiny steps on the carpet, his hands in front of him and his great big wet handkerchief flapping in one hand.

Now it's getting narrow, I said. Look out for yourself and try to jump to that pale flower in the centre!

The flower was almost right behind him and the pattern disappeared in a twirl. He tried desperately to keep his balance, flapped his handkerchief and began to scream, and then fell into the dark part. He screamed and screamed and rolled over on the carpet, rolled off onto the floor and under a cupboard. I screamed too, crawled after him and put my arms round him and held him tight until he calmed down.

People shouldn't have pile carpets, they're dangerous. It's much better to live in a studio with a concrete floor. That's why Poyu is always longing to come to our place.

We are busy digging a secret tunnel through the wall. I've got quite a long way and I only work when I'm alone. The wooden panelling went all right but then I had to use the marble hammer. Poyu's hole is much smaller but his Daddy's tools are so bad that it's a disgrace.

Every time I'm alone I take down the hanging on the wall and dig away and no one has noticed what I am doing. The hanging is Mummy's. She painted it on sack-cloth when she was young. It shows an evening. There are straight tree-trunks rising out of the moss and behind the tree-trunks the sky is red because the sun is setting. Everything except the sky has gone dark in a vague greyish brown but

there are narrow red streaks that burn like fire. I love her picture. It goes deep into the wall, deeper than my hole, deeper than Poyu's drawing-room, it goes on endlessly and one never gets to the place where the sun is setting but the red gets more and more intense. I'm sure it's burning! There is a terrible fire, the kind of fire Daddy is always going out and waiting for.

The first time Daddy showed me his fire it was winter. He went across the ice first and Mummy came behind him, pulling me on a sledge. It was the same red sky and the same shadowy figures running and something terrible had happened. There were jagged black things lying on the ice. Daddy collected them together and placed them in my lap, they were very heavy and pressed against my tummy.

Explosion is a beautiful word and a very big one. Later I learned others, the kind you can whisper only when you're alone. Inexorable. Ornamentation. Profile. Catastrophic. Electrical. District Nurse.

They get bigger and bigger if you say them over and over again. You whisper and whisper and let the word grow until nothing exists except the word.

I wonder why fires always happen at night. Perhaps Daddy isn't interested in fires during the daytime because then the sky isn't red. He always woke us up and we heard the fire engine clanging, there was always a great rush and we ran through completely empty streets. It was always an awful long way to Daddy's fires. All the houses were asleep and the pointed chimneys were lifted upwards towards the red sky which got nearer and nearer and at last we got there and Daddy lifted me up to see the fire. But sometimes it was a silly little fire that had already gone out long before we got there and then he was disappointed and had to be consoled.

Mummy only likes little fires like the ones she makes in ashtrays when no one is looking. And log-fires. She lights log-fires in the studio and in the passage every evening after Daddy has gone out looking for his friends.

When the log-fire is alight we draw up the big chair. We turn out the lights in the studio and sit in front of the fire and she says: once upon a time there was a little girl who was terribly pretty and her mummy liked her so awfully much … Every story has to begin in the same way, then it's not so important what happens. A soft, gentle voice in the warm darkness and one gazes into the fire and nothing is dangerous. Everything else is outside and can't get in. Not now or at any time.

My Mummy has lots of dark hair and it falls round you like a cloud, it smells nice and is like the hair of the sad queens in the book. The most beautiful picture covers a whole page. It shows a landscape at twilight, a plain covered with lilies. Pale queens are wandering over the whole plain with watering cans. The nearest one is indescribably beautiful. Her long dark hair is as soft as a

cloud and the artist has covered it with sequins, probably some special finishing coat when the rest was done. Her profile is gentle and grave. And she walks there watering for the whole of her life and no one really knows how beautiful and how sad she is. The watering cans are painted with real silver and how the publisher could afford such a thing neither Mummy nor I can understand.

Mummy's stories are often about Moses – in the bulrushes and later; about Isaac and about people who are homesick for their own country or get lost and then find their way again; about Eve and the Serpent in Paradise and great storms that die away in the end. Most of the people are homesick anyway, and a little lonely, and they hide themselves in their hair and are turned into flowers. Sometimes they are turned into frogs and God keeps an eye on them the whole time and forgives them when he isn't angry and hurt and destroying whole cities because they believe in other gods.

Moses couldn't always control himself either. But the women just waited and longed for their homes. Oh I will lead you to your own country or to whatever country in the world you want and paint sequins in your hair and build a castle for you where we shall live until we die and never never leave each other. Through endless forest dark and drear no comfort near a little girl alone did roam so far from home the way was long the night was cold the thunder rolled the girl did weep no more

I'll find my mother kind for in this lonely haunted spot my awful lot will be beneath this tree to lie and slowly die.

Very satisfying. That's how it was when we shut the danger out.

Daddy's statues moved slowly round us in the light from the fire, his sad white ladies stepping warily, all ready to escape. They knew about the danger that lies in wait everywhere but nothing could save them until they were carved in marble and placed in a museum. There one is safe. In a museum or in a lap or in a tree. Perhaps under the bedclothes. But the best thing of all is to sit high up in a tree, that is if one isn't still inside one's Mummy's tummy.

The Stone

IT WAS LYING BETWEEN the coal dump and the goods wagons under some bits of wood and it was a miracle that no one had found it before me. The whole of one side shone with silver and if you rubbed away the coal dust you could see that the silver was there inside the stone too. It was a huge stone of nothing but silver and no one had found it.

I didn't dare to hide it, somebody might see it and take it while I ran home. It had to be rolled away. If anyone came and tried to stop me I would sit down on the stone and yell my head off. I could bite them as they tried to lift it. I could do just anything.

And so I began to roll it. It was very slow work. The stone just lay on its back quite still and when I got it to turn over it just lay on its tummy and rocked to and fro. The silver came off in thin flakes that stuck to the ground and broke into small pieces when I tried to pick them up.

I got down on my knees to roll it, which was much better. But the stone only moved half a turn at a time and it was terribly slow work. No one took any notice of me as long as I was rolling down in the harbour. Then I managed to get the stone onto a pavement and things became more difficult. People stopped and tapped on the pavement with their umbrellas and said all sorts of things. I said nothing and just looked at their shoes. I pulled my woolly hat down over my eyes and just went on rolling and rolling and rolling and then the stone had to cross the road. By then I had been rolling it for hours and I hadn't looked up once and hadn't listened to anything anyone said to me. I just gazed at the silver underneath all the coal dust and other dirt and made a tiny little room for myself where nothing existed except the stone and me. But now it had to cross the road.

One car after another went past and sometimes a tram and the longer I waited the more difficult it was to roll the stone out into the road.

In the end I began to feel weak at the knees and then I knew that soon it would be too late, in a few seconds it would be too late, so I let it fall into the gutter and began rolling very quickly and without looking up. I kept my nose just above the top of the stone so that the room I had hidden us in would be as tiny as possible and I heard very clearly how all the cars stopped and were angry but I drew a line between them and me and just went on rolling and rolling. You can close your mind to things if something is important enough. It works very well. You make yourself very small, shut your eyes tight and say a big word over and over again until you're safe.

When I got to the tram-lines I felt tired so I lay across the stone and held it tight. But the tram just rang and rang its bell so I had to start rolling again but now I wasn't scared any longer, just angry and that felt much better. Anyway, the stone and I had such a tiny room for ourselves that it didn't matter a bit who shouted at us or what they shouted. We felt terribly strong. We had no trouble in getting onto the pavement again and we continued up the slope to Wharf Road, leaving behind us a narrow trail of silver. From time to time we stopped to rest together and then we went on again.

We came to the entrance of our house and got the door open. But then there were the stairs. You could manage by resting on your knees and taking a firm grip with both hands and waiting till you got your balance. Then you tightened your stomach and held your breath and pressed your wrists against your knees. Then quickly up and over the edge and you let your stomach go again and listened and waited but the staircase was quite empty. And then the same thing all over again.

When the stairs narrowed and turned a corner we had to move over to the wall side. We went on climbing slowly but no one came. Then I lay on top of the stone again and got my breath and looked at the silver, silver worth millions and only four floors more and we would be there.

It happened when we got to the fourth floor. My hand slipped inside my mittens, I fell flat on my face and lay quite still and listened to the terrible noise of the stone falling. The noise got louder and louder, a noise like Crash, Crunch, Crack all rolled into one, until the stone hit the Nieminens' door with a dull thud like doomsday.

It was the end of the world, and I covered my eyes with my mittens. Nothing happened. The echoes resounded up and down the stairs but nothing happened. No angry people opened their doors. Perhaps they were lying in wait inside.

I crept down on my hands and knees. Every step had a little semicircle bitten out of it. Further down they became big semicircles and the pieces lay everywhere and stared back at me. I rolled the stone away from the Nieminens' door and started all over again. We climbed up steadily and without looking at the chipped steps. We got past the place where things had gone wrong and took a rest in front of the balcony door. It's a dark-brown door and has tiny square panes of glass.

Then I heard the outside door downstairs open and shut and somebody coming up the stairs. He climbed up and up with very slow steps. I crept forward to the banisters and looked down. I could see right to the bottom, a long narrow rectangle

closed in by the banisters all the way down, and up the banisters came a great big hand, round and round and nearer and nearer. There was a mark in the middle of it so I knew it was the tattooed hand of the caretaker who was probably on his way up to the attic.

I opened the door to the balcony as quietly as I could and began to roll the stone over the threshold. The threshold was high. I rolled without thinking, I was very scared and couldn't get a good grasp and the stone rolled into the chink of the door and got wedged there. There were double doors with coiled iron springs at the top which the caretaker had put there because women always forgot to shut the doors after them. I heard the springs contract and they sang softly to themselves as they squeezed me and the stone together between the doors and I put my legs together and took tight hold of the stone and tried to roll it but the space got narrower and narrower and I knew that the caretaker's hand was sliding up the banisters all the time.

I saw the silver of the stone quite close to my face and I gripped it and pushed and kicked with my legs and all of a sudden it tipped over and rolled several times and under the iron railing and into the air and disappeared.

Then I could see nothing but bits of fluff, light and airy as down, with small threads of colour here and there. I lay flat on my tummy and the door pinched my neck and everything was quiet until the stone reached the yard below. And there it exploded like a meteor, it covered the dustbins and the washing and all the steps and windows with silver! It made the whole of 4 Wharf Road look as if it was silver-plated and all the women ran to their windows thinking that war had broken out or doomsday had come! Every door opened and everybody ran up and down the stairs with the caretaker leading and saw how a wild animal had bitten bits out of every step and how a meteor had fallen out of a clear blue sky.

But I lay squeezed in between the doors and said nothing. I didn't say anything afterwards either. I never told anyone how close we had come to being rich.

Parties

SOMETIMES I WAS WOKEN UP in the middle of the night by the most beautiful music there is, balalaika and guitar. Daddy played the balalaika and Cavvy played the guitar. They played together very softly, almost in a whisper, both of them a long way away and then they sounded a little closer in turns so that sometimes it was the guitar that I heard and sometimes the balalaika.

They were gentle, sad songs about things that go on and on and that nobody can do anything about. Then they became wild and disorderly and Marcus broke his glass. But he never smashed more than one and Daddy made sure that he was always given one of the cheaper sort. Below the ceiling near my bed on the top bunk there was a cloud of grey tobacco smoke, and it made everything more unreal than it was. Perhaps we were out at sea or up in the mountains and I heard them shouting to each other through the cloud and things kept falling over and behind the violent noises came loud and soft waves of balalaika and guitar music.

I love Daddy's parties. They could go on for many nights of waking up and going to sleep again and being rocked by smoke and the music and then suddenly a bellow would strike a chill right down to my toes.

It's not worth looking because if you do everything you've imagined disappears. It's always the same. You can look down on them and there they are sitting on the sofa or on chairs or walking slowly up and down the room. Cavvy sits huddled up over his guitar as if he was hiding in it, his bald head floating around like a pale spot in the cloud and he sinks lower and lower. Daddy sits very upright and looks straight ahead. The others doze off from time to time because having a party is very exhausting. But they won't go home because it's very important to make an effort to be the last. Daddy generally wins and is last. When all the others are asleep he goes on staring and thinking till morning.

Mummy doesn't join in the party. She sees that the oil lamp doesn't start smoking in the bedroom. The bedroom is our only real room apart from the kitchen, I mean it has a door. But there is no stove in it. So the oil lamp must burn all night. If the door is opened the smoke gets into the bedroom and Per Olov gets asthma. Parties have been much more difficult since I got a brother but Mummy and Daddy try their best to arrange them all the same.

The table is the most beautiful thing. Sometimes I sit up and look over the railing and screw up my eyes and then the glasses and the candles and all the things on the table shimmer and make a whole as they do in a painting. Making a whole is very important. Some people just paint things and forget the whole, I know. I know a lot that I don't talk about.

All men have parties and are pals who never let each other down. A pal can say terrible things which are forgotten the next day. A pal never forgives, he just forgets and a woman forgives but never forgets. That's how it is. That's why women aren't allowed to have parties. Being forgiven is very unpleasant.

A pal never says anything clever that's worth repeating the following day. He just feels that nothing is so important at the time.

Once Daddy and Cavvy played with a catapult that could shoot aeroplanes. I don't think Cavvy understood how it worked because he did it wrong and the aeroplane flew straight at his hand and the hook went right through it. It was awful and the blood ran all over the table and he couldn't even get his jacket on because the aeroplane wouldn't go through his sleeve. Daddy consoled him and took him to the hospital where they snipped off the hook with pincers and put the aeroplane in the museum.

Anything can happen at a party if you aren't careful.

We never had a party in the studio, only in the living room. There are two high windows there which have a solemn-looking arch at the top and the whole of Grandmother's and Grandfather's curly-grained suite with scrolls all over it is there. It reminds Mummy of the house in the country where everything is just as it should be.

At first she was worried about the suite and was cross because of the cigarette burns and the marks left by glasses but by now she knows that it's all a question of patina.

Mummy is very good about parties. She never puts everything on the table and she never invites people. She knows that the only thing that really creates the right atmosphere is improvisation. Improvisation is a beautiful word. Daddy has to go out and look for his pals. They might be anywhere at any time. Sometimes he doesn't find anybody. But often he does. And then they feel like going somewhere. One always lands up somewhere. That's important.

Then someone says let's look and see what we can find in the pantry. And one goes quietly to have a look and there's lots there! One finds expensive sausages and bottles and loaves of bread and butter and cheese and even soda water and then one carries everything in and improvises something. Mummy has everything ready.

Actually, soda water is dangerous. It gives one bubbles in the tummy and it can make one feel very sad. One should never mix things.

Gradually all the candles on the balustrade go out and candlewax runs down onto the sofa. When the music is finished there are war stories. Then I wait under the bedclothes but I always come up again when they attack the wicker chair. Then Daddy goes and fetches his bayonet which hangs above the sacks of plaster in the studio and everybody jumps up and shouts and Daddy attacks the chair. During the day it is covered with a rug so that you can't see what it looks like. After the wicker chair Daddy doesn't want to play his balalaika any more. Then I just go to sleep.

The next day everybody is still there and they try to say nice things to me. Good-day pretty maiden, how lovely 'twould be if you'd come a-walking this morning with me. Mummy gets presents. Ruokokoski once gave her half a pound of butter and another time she got a dozen eggs from Sallinen.

In the morning it's very important not to begin to tidy up too obviously. And if one lets in all that nasty fresh air anyone can catch cold or get depressed. It's important to break the new day in very gradually and gently. Things look different in daylight and if the difference seems too sudden everything can be spoilt. One must be able to move about in peace and quiet and see how one feels and wonder what it is one really wants to do.

One always wants something the next day but one doesn't really know what. Finally one thinks that perhaps it's pickled herring. And so one goes into the pantry and has another look and there really is some pickled herring there.

And so the day goes on quietly and it's evening again and perhaps there are some new candles. Everyone behaves terribly cautiously because they know how little it takes to upset everything.

I go to bed and hear Daddy tuning his balalaika. Mummy lights the oil lamp. There's a completely round window in the bedroom. Nobody else has a round window. One can see out across all the roofs and over the harbour and gradually all the windows go dark except one. It is the one under Victor Ek's asbestos wall. There's a light on there all night. I think they're having a party there too. Or perhaps they're illustrating books.

Annie

IT WAS SO NICE LOOKING AT ANNIE. Her hair grew like luscious rough grass, it looked as if it had been cut any old how and was so full of life that it crackled. Her eyebrows were just as thick and black and met in the middle, her nose was flat and she had very pink cheeks. Her arms plunged into the washing-up water like pillars. She was beautiful.

Annie sings while she's washing up and I sit under the table and try to learn the words. I've got to the thirteenth verse of Lord Henry and Fair Hilda and that's where things actually start to happen.

The sound of a charger was heard in the hall and harpist and fiddler and wedding guests all were filled with such horror for yea it is told Lord Henry rode in clad as warrior bold. Lo! vengeance be mine and in blood for this day oh Hilda so fair you our love do betray pale ghost of a bride on your penitent knee the wrath of my upraisèd arm you shall see. It makes you shiver it's so beautiful. It's the same for Annie when she says: you must go out for a while because I want to cry it's so beautiful.

Annie's lovers often come clad as warriors bold. I liked the dragoon in red trousers with gold braid on his jacket, he was so handsome. He took off his sword. Sometimes it fell on the floor and I could hear it rattle from all the way up on my bunk – and thought of the wrath of his upraisèd arm. Then he disappeared and Annie got another lover who was a Thinking Man. So she went to listen to Plato and despised Daddy because he read newspapers and Mummy because she read novels.

I explained to Annie that Mummy had no time to read any books other than those she had to draw the jackets for so that she could find out what the book was about and what the heroine looked like. Some people just draw as they like and don't give a fig for the author. That's wrong. An illustrator has to think of the author and the reader and sometimes even of the publisher.

Huh! said Annie. It's a rubbishy old firm that doesn't publish Plato. Anyway, everything the mistress draws for she gets free and on the last jacket the heroine didn't have yellow hair although it was yellow in the book.

Colour is expensive! I said and got angry. Anyhow, she has to pay fifty per cent for some of the books! It was impossible to explain to Annie that publishers don't like to print in many colours and that they go on about two-colour printing although they know

that one of the colours must be black anyway and that one can draw hair without using yellow and make it look yellow all the same.

Is that so? said Annie. And what has that to do with Plato if I might ask?

Then I forgot what it was I had to say. Annie always got things mixed up and was always right in the end.

But sometimes I bullied her. I made her tell me about her childhood until she started to cry and then I just stood in the window, rocking backwards and forwards on my heels and staring down at the yard. Or I stopped asking questions although her face was swollen and she threw the dustpan right across the kitchen. I could bully Annie by being polite to her lovers and asking them questions about things that interested them and just not going away and leaving them alone. And a very good way was to put on a haughty drawling voice and say: the mistress wants roast veal on Sunday, and then leave immediately as if Annie and I had nothing else to say to each other.

Annie got her revenge with Plato for a long time. Once she had a lover who was a Man of the People, and then she got her revenge by talking about all the old women who got up at four o'clock in the morning to deliver newspapers while the master lay lounging in bed waiting for the morning paper. I said that no old woman in the world who delivered newspapers worked all night making a plaster cast for a competition and that Mummy worked till two o'clock every night while Annie lay in bed lounging and then Annie said don't mix me up in all this and anyway the master didn't get a prize last time! Then I shouted that it was because the jury had been unfair and she shouted that it was easy to say that and I said that she didn't understand a thing about it because she wasn't an artist and she said that it was all very well to get all superior when some people hadn't even been taught to draw and so we didn't speak to each other for several hours.

When we had both had a good cry I went into the kitchen again and Annie had hung a blanket over the kitchen table. This meant that I was allowed to play houses under the table provided that I didn't get in her way or block the pantry door. I built my house with logs and chairs and stools. I only did it out of politeness because actually you could build a much better house under the big modelling stand in the studio.

When the house was ready she gave me some crockery. I took this out of politeness too. I don't like pretending to cook. I hate food.

Once there was no bird-cherry in the market for the first of June. Mummy has to have bird-cherry for her birthday otherwise she will die. That's what a gipsy told her when she was fifteen years old and since then everyone has always made a terrible fuss about bird-cherry. Sometimes it comes out too early and sometimes too late. If you bring it into the house in the middle of May it goes brown round the edges and the flowers never really come out.

But Annie said: I know there is a white bird-cherry in the park. We'll go and pick some when it gets dark.

It was terribly late when it got dark but I was allowed to go with her in any case and we didn't say a word about what we were going to do. Annie took my hand; her hands are always damp and warm and as she moved there was a smell about her that was hot and a little frightening. We went down Wharf Road and across to the park and I was scared stiff and thought about the park keeper and the Town Council and God.

Daddy would never do anything like this, I said.

No he wouldn't, Annie said, the master's far too bourgeois. You just help yourself to what you want, and that's all there is to it.

We had climbed over the fence before I had really grasped the unthinkable thing she had said about Daddy being bourgeois. I was so taken aback that I didn't have time to be offended.

Annie strode up to the white bush in the middle of the grass and began picking. You're doing it wrong! I hissed. Do it properly!

Annie stood upright in the grass with her legs apart and looked at me. She opened her big mouth and laughed so that you could see all her beautiful white teeth and she took me by the hand again and crouched down and we ran under the bushes and began to creep away. We sneaked up to another white bush and Annie was looking over her shoulder the whole time and sometimes she stopped behind a tree. Is it better this way? she asked.

I nodded and squeezed her hand. Then she started picking again. She reached up with her enormous arms so that her dress stretched tight all over and she laughed and broke off the boughs and the flowers rained all over her face and I whispered stop, stop, that's enough, and I was so beside myself with fright and ecstasy that I almost wet my knickers.

If you're going to steal you might as well steal properly, Annie said calmly. Her arms were full of bird-cherry, it lay across her neck and shoulders and she clasped it firmly with her red hands. We climbed back over the fence and went home and there was no sign of a park keeper or a policeman.

Then they told us that the bush we had picked from wasn't a bird-cherry at all. It was just white. But Mummy was all right, she didn't die.

Sometimes Annie would get mad and shout: I can't stand the sight of you! Get out! Then I would go down into the yard and sit on the rubbish bin and burn old rolls of film with a magnifying glass.

I love smells. The smell of burning films, the smell of heat and Annie and the box of clay in the studio and Mummy's hair and the smell of parties and bird-cherry. I haven't got a smell yet, at least I don't think so.

Annie smelt differently in the summer – of grass and even warmer. She laughed more often and you could see more of her arms and legs.

Annie could really row. She took a single pull and then rested on the oars in triumph and the boat glided forward over the sound so that there was a splashing round the bows in the still water of evening and then she took another pull and the boat splashed again and Annie showed how strong she was. Then she would laugh loudly and put one oar in the water so that the boat swung round to show that she didn't want to go in any particular direction but was just amusing herself. In the end she just let the boat drift and lay in the bottom and sang and everybody on the shore heard her singing in the sunset and they knew that there she lay, big and happy and warm and not caring a fig for anything. She was doing just what she wanted to do.

Then she would stroll up the slope, her whole body swaying to and fro, and now and then she would pause to pick a flower. Annie used to sing when she was baking, too. She kneaded the dough, rolled it out, patted it, shaped it and threw her buns into the oven so that they landed exactly in the right place on the tray and then she slammed the oven door and cried, oh! it's so hot!

I love Annie in the summer and never bully her then.

Sometimes we went to Diamond Valley. It's a beach where all the pebbles are round and precious and beautiful colours. They're prettier under the water but if you rub them with margarine they're always pretty. We went there once when Mummy and Daddy were working in town and when we had gathered enough diamonds we sat and rested on the hill slope. In the early summer and autumn there are always streams coming down the slope. We made waterfalls and dams.

There's gold in the stream, Annie said. See if you can find it. I couldn't see any gold.

You have to put it there yourself, said Annie. Gold looks wonderful in brown water. It multiplies. More and more gold. So I went home and fetched all the gold things we possessed and the pearls as well, and put them all in the stream and they looked terribly beautiful.

Annie and I lay in the grass and listened to the sound of the stream and she sang Full Fathom Five. She stepped into the water and picked up Mummy's gold bracelet with her toes and dropped it again and laughed. Then she said: I've always longed to have things of real gold.

Next day all the gold had disappeared and the pearls too. I thought it was odd. You never know what streams will do, Annie said. Sometimes the gold grows and grows and sometimes it vanishes under the ground. But it can come up again if you don't talk about it. So we went home and made some pancakes.

In the evening Annie went to meet her new lover at the village swing. He was a Man of Action and could make the swing go right round and the only person who dared to sit on it while it went round four times was Annie.

The Iceberg

THE SUMMER CAME SO EARLY that year that it might almost have been called spring – it was a kind of present and everything one did had to be thought out differently. It was cloudy and very calm.

We and our luggage were the same as usual, and so were Old Charlie and Old Charlie's boat, but the beaches were bare and forbidding and the sea looked stern. And when we had rowed as far as Newness Island the iceberg came floating towards us.

It was green and white and sparkling and it was coming in order to meet me. I had never seen an iceberg before.

Now it all depended on whether anyone said anything. If they said a single word about the iceberg it wouldn't be mine any longer.

We got closer and closer. Daddy rested on his oars but Old Charlie went on rowing and said: it's early this year. And Daddy answered: yes. It's not long since it broke up, and went on rowing.

Mummy didn't say a thing.

Anyway, you couldn't count that as actually saying anything about an iceberg and so this iceberg *was* mine.

We rowed past it but I didn't turn round to look because then they might have said something. I just thought about it all the way along Batch Island. My iceberg looked like a tattered crown. On one side there was an oval-shaped grotto which was very green and closed in by a grating of ice. Under the water the ice was a different green which went very deep down and was almost black where the dangerous depths began. I knew that the iceberg would follow me and I wasn't the least bit worried about it.

I sat in the bay all day long and waited. Evening came but still the iceberg hadn't reached me. I said nothing, and no one asked me anything. They were all busy unpacking.

When I went to bed the wind had got up. I lay under the bedclothes and imagined I was an ice-mermaid listening to the wind rising. It was important not to fall asleep but I did anyway, and when I woke up the house was completely quiet. Then I got up and dressed and took Daddy's torch and went out onto the steps.

It was a light night, but it was the first time I had been out alone at night and I thought about the iceberg all the time so that I wouldn't get frightened. I didn't light the torch. The landscape was just as forbidding as before and looked like an illustration in which for once they had printed the grey shades properly. Out at sea the long-tailed ducks were carrying on like mad, singing wedding songs to one another.

Even before I got to the field by the shore I could see the iceberg. It was waiting for me and was shining just as beautifully but very faintly. It was lying there bumping against the rocks at the end of the point where it was deep, and there was deep black water and just the wrong distance between us. If it had been shorter I should have jumped over, if it had been a little longer I could have thought: what a pity, no one can manage to get over that.

Now I had to make up my mind. And that's an awful thing to have to do.

The oval grotto with the grating of ice was facing the shore and the grotto was as big as me. It was made for a little girl who pulled up her legs and cuddled them to her. There was room for the torch too.

I lay down flat on the rock, reached out with my hand and broke off one of the icicles in the grating. It was so cold it felt hot. I held on to the grating with both hands and could feel it melting. The iceberg was moving as one does when one breathes – it was trying to come to me.

My hands and my tummy began to feel icy cold and I sat up. The grotto was the same size as me, but I didn't dare to jump. And if one doesn't dare to do something immediately then one never does it.

I switched on the torch and threw it into the grotto. It fell on its side and lit up the whole grotto, making it just as beautiful as I had imagined it would be. It became an illuminated aquarium at night, the manger at Bethlehem or the biggest emerald in the world! It was so unbearably beautiful that I had to get away from the whole thing as quickly as possible, send it away, *do something*! So I sat down firmly and placed both feet on the iceberg and pushed it as hard as I could. It didn't move.

Go away! I shouted. Clear off!

And then the iceberg glided very slowly away from me and was caught by the off-shore wind. I was so cold that I ached and saw the iceberg carried by the wind towards the sound – it would sail right out to sea with Daddy's torch on board and the ducks would sing themselves hoarse when they saw an illuminated bridal barge coming towards them.

And so my honour was saved.

When I got to the steps I turned round and looked. My iceberg shone steadily out there like a green beacon and the batteries would last until sunrise because they were always new when one had just moved to the country. Perhaps they would last another night, perhaps the torch would go on shining at the bottom of the sea after the iceberg had melted and turned into water.

I got into bed and pulled the bedclothes over my head and waited for the warmth to come back. It came. Slowly at first, but little by little it reached down to my feet.

But all the same I had been a coward, and all because of two inches. I could feel it in my tummy. Sometimes I think all strong feelings start in the tummy; for me they do at any rate.

The Bays

THE HOUSE IS GREY, the sky and the sea are grey, and the field is grey with dew. It's four o'clock in the morning and I have saved three important hours which can be counted as extra. Or perhaps three and a half.

I have learned to tell the time, although I'm not yet quite sure about the minutes.

I'm also light grey, but inside, because I'm all vague and wobbly like a jelly-fish, not thinking but just feeling. If you sailed a hundred miles over the sea and walked a hundred miles through the forest in all directions, you wouldn't find a little girl at all. They just don't exist. I know because I've found out. You can wait for them for a thousand years and they just don't exist. The nearest thing to it you'll find is Fanny who is almost seventy and collects pebbles and shells and dead animals and sings when it's going to rain. She's yellowish-grey just like the trampled scorched grass round the house, her face, her dress and her hands, everything about her is yellowish-grey and wrinkled but her hair is white and her eyes are whitish-blue and look straight past you.

Fanny is the only person who isn't afraid of the horses. She shouts at them and turns her backside to them, and she does just what she likes. If anyone asks her to do the washing-up in the wrong tone of voice she goes into the forest and stays there for several days and nights and sings to make it rain.

She's never lonely.

There are five bays where no one lives. Once you've been round the first you have to go into the second. The first is wide and full of white sand. It has a grotto with a sandy floor. The walls are always wet and there is a narrow opening in the roof. The grotto is longer than I am when I lie on my back and today it is icy cold. There is a narrow black hole right inside.

It was then that my secret friend crept out of the hole.

I said: what a beautiful and extremely pleasant morning it is.

And he answered: it's no ordinary morning because I heard rumbling below the horizon.

He sat down behind me and I knew that he had changed his skin and didn't want me to look at him. So I said rather indifferently: it rumbled on Friday, too. Have you seen Fanny?

She was sitting in a rowan tree just before dusk, he answered. But I knew that Fanny didn't really

like climbing trees and that he was just trying to impress me. So I didn't say anything and just let him be. It was nice to have someone's company. When he noticed that I didn't feel like talking he played for me a while. It was icy cold in the grotto and I decided to leave as soon as he had finished playing. So after the last verse I said: that was an agreeable visit. But I'm afraid I shall have to leave. How are things at home?

Fine, he answered. My wife has just had quintuplets. All of them girls.

I congratulated him and went on my way.

When the sun rises in the first bay the water is in the shade of the forest but at the entrance to the bay the rocks are red. The seaweed only shines in the evening. You walk and walk and walk and the morning wind begins to get up. The second bay is full of reeds and when the wind blows through them they rustle, and swish and sigh and whisper and whine softly and gently and you go right into the reeds and they brush you on all sides and you go on and on, thinking of nothing at all. The reeds are a jungle that goes on and on right to the end of the earth. The face of the earth is covered by nothing but whispering reeds and all human beings have died and I am the only one left and I just walk on and on through the reeds.

I walk for such a long time that I become tall and thin like a reed and my hair becomes its soft feathery panicle until in the end I take root and begin to swish and rush and sigh like all my reed sisters and time becomes endless.

But in the bay sat a great big pilot who said: ha! ha! ha! ha! The wind is turning westerly I wouldn't be surprised. He had a red moustache and blue eyes and was wearing pilot's uniform and had at last noticed me.

I was trembling with joy and answered: force nine I should think, if not more. Would you like a little snorter?

Well, no one likes to see good stuff going begging, he answered, and held out his glass.

I filled it five times.

And what do you think of the pike? he went on.

They'll rise, I said. If this wind holds . . .

He nodded thoughtfully and appreciatively. I dare say, he said. They might well.

We drank six quarts of home-brew and two buckets of strong coffee.

Then I said: It's a bad time for pilots, isn't it?

Could be, could be, he answered.

Then I couldn't keep him there any longer.

It's awful when they go all misty and vanish. You say all the right things but they disappear all the same. It's not worth going on with it then because it seems silly and you begin to feel lonely.

Now I am in the third bay.

It was here that Daddy and I found our first canisters. It was a day that neither of us will forget as long as we live.

Daddy saw at once what it was. He stood rooted to the spot and craned his neck. He balanced himself out on the stones and began to haul it in. It was an old rotten sack but you could hear the canisters rattling inside it and Daddy said: did you hear that? Did you hear the noise it's making?

There were four canisters in the sack with two gallons of ninety-six per cent alcohol in each. Oh Daddy, Daddy! And just at that moment the Herberts came round the point. We lay down flat behind the stones very close to one another. I held Daddy's hand. The Herberts took up their long-lines and didn't notice a thing. Daddy and I watched them until the danger was over and then we hid the canisters in the seaweed.

I always sit quite still for a long while in the third bay in memory of the time when Daddy and I came across our great secret.

The sun is higher in the sky and everything is beginning to look normal. It'll be more difficult to find company now – they're only around early in the morning and at dusk. But it doesn't matter. I can keep my eyes shut and think about the past instead.

I'm thinking about the time when Daddy and I walked through the forest with the storm-lantern to fetch the baskets of mushrooms.

During the day the family had picked them. Daddy had led us to the right places, his places, where crowds of mushrooms grew. He didn't pick any himself, he just lit his pipe and made a gesture which seemed to say, carry on everybody. Food!

We picked and picked. Not just any old how. Mushrooms were important – hundreds of lunches during the whole winter. Almost as important as fish. Every mushroom has mysterious mycelia under it and the place where they grow must be preserved for ever and ever for future generations and it is a sign of good citizenship to collect food for one's family in the summer and to show respect for nature.

At night it's quite different. Then Daddy and I carry the baskets of mushrooms home that we couldn't manage during the day. It has to be dark. There was no need to save oil, so we were really extravagant with it. And Daddy always found the place. Sometimes it was windy and the branches made a ghastly sound as they rubbed against each other. Daddy found the right spot. There were the baskets of mushrooms and he said: well I'll be damned! Look, there they are!

The most beautiful mushrooms were on top. He arranged them according to their colour and shape because they were his bouquets. He did the same with fish.

Once Daddy put his baskets of mushrooms down on the ground and went into the house to find the rest of the family. While he was inside Rosa the cow devoured the lot. She knew she could rely on Daddy and that there wasn't a single poisonous mushroom in the basket.

Now there's a steady wind. The fourth bay is a long way away. I am going through a forest drawn by that great artist John Bauer. He knew how to draw forests and since he was drowned nobody has dared to draw them. And Mummy and I think that anybody who does is contemptible.

To draw a forest so that it's big enough you don't include the tops of the trees or any sky. Just very thick tree-trunks growing absolutely straight. The ground consists of soft mounds, getting farther and farther away and smaller and smaller until the forest becomes endless. There are stones but you can't see them. Moss has grown over them for thousands of years and no one has disturbed it. If you step on the moss once you make a big hole which doesn't straighten out for a week. If you step on it a second time there will be a hole there for ever and ever. The third time you step on the moss it will die.

In a proper painting of a forest everything is roughly the same colour, the moss, the tree-trunks and the branches of the fir trees, everything is soft and solemn, half-way between grey and brown and green, but very little green. If you want you can add a princess, for example. She is always white and very tiny and has long yellow hair. She is placed in the middle or in the golden section. After John Bauer's death princesses became modern and were just any colour. They were just ordinary children dressed up.

It's the fourth bay that is the great carcass bay where the pig floated ashore. It was enormous and smelt terrible. Sometimes I think it was an awful-reddish-blue colour and its eyes rolled as it was dashed against the rocks but I'm not sure and I don't care to think about it too much.

You never meet anybody in the great carcass bay and there's nothing to remember. It's a place for awful images that rise up out of the sea.

First come the birds. You can see them on the horizon like a bank of clouds. The cloud gets bigger. Great birds thirty feet long flying so slowly it's uncanny. Their wings look like tattered palm leaves, straggling and blown to shreds, a thousand enormous birds stretch across the sky casting shadows over the earth. Not one of them says a thing.

And now ...

If a morning came when the sun didn't rise. If we were to wake up as usual and Daddy looked at the clock and said: now it's gone wrong again. Clocks are inventions of the devil! We tried to go to sleep again, but we couldn't. Daddy tried to get something on the wireless, but it just whined. Then we went out to see if anything had happened to the earth lead. It looked just as it should. The aerial was still there in the birch tree. It was eight o'clock but still completely dark. As we all felt wide awake we had a cup of tea. Fanny was sitting on the fence singing the great rain song.

It was nine o'clock, ten, eleven and then twelve, but the sun did not rise and it stayed dark. Then Daddy said, well, dammit, something's wrong. So he went and talked to Old Charlie for a while. Old Charlie was taking his fishing-nets up and said the weather's sure to change somehow. This sort of thing hasn't been seen in living memory.

It was as silent as during an eclipse of the sun. And it was cold, too. Mummy carried in some wood and lit the fire. Then it was two o'clock and three o'clock and four o'clock. It was seventy-five minutes past six. Then Mummy said: we have two packets of candles and half a gallon of oil. But then who knows what will happen to us.

And just then there was a rumbling below the horizon.

That was a good story. Another one.

One evening just before dusk we heard a faint gurgling sound. When we went out to see what it was we saw that the sea had subsided fifteen feet and the beach was green and slimy. The boats were strangling themselves with their painters. The perch in the fish-cage were jumping about like mad. Empty bottles and old tins crept up out of the sea and looked ashamed of themselves. The sea went on falling. There were bubbles round Red Rock as the sea slunk down into the cod-bank. The sea crept further and further out and sank lower and lower revealing hundreds of old skeletons, dead pigs and unmentionable things.

Unmentionable things. It couldn't be worse than that.

Suddenly I was fed up with everything.

You can jump from one stone to another. That is you must jump very quickly and only touch each stone for a second. You must never step on to the seaweed or the sand, only on the stones, faster and faster. In the end you become a wind, the wind itself, and it whistles in your ears and everything else is wiped out and vanished, there is only the wind and jumping and jumping and jumping. I never make a false jump, I'm confident and strong and I go on jumping until I come to the last bay which is tiny and beautiful and all my own. Here is the climbing tree with branches all the way up like Jacob's Ladder and at the top the whole pine tree is swaying because the wind is now coming from the south-west. The sun has come up in time for breakfast.

If a thousand little girls walked past under this tree not one of them would have the faintest idea that I am sitting up here. The pine cones are green and very hard. My feet are brown. And the wind is blowing right through my hair.

Flotsam and Jetsam

IF THE WATER RISES THERE'LL BE A STORM. If it falls very quickly and sharply there might be a storm too. A ring around the sun may be dangerous. And a smoky, dark-red sunset bodes no good either. There are many more things like this, but I can't be bothered with them just now. If it's not one thing then it's another.

In the end, Daddy couldn't put up with being uneasy about the weather and set off. He set the spritsail and said, now remember that one mustn't have a single unnecessary thing in a boat.

We sat still. We weren't allowed to read because that shows a lack of respect for the boat. You couldn't trail anything in the water, such as painters or boats of bark because the pilots might see them. We gave the sandbank a fairly wide berth, but not too narrow because that's asking for trouble and not too wide because that looks too cautious and the pilots might see it. Then we were on our way.

There are lots of things to attend to in a boat. You have to watch out for the painter otherwise it gets tangled round your feet and can pull you overboard. You might slip when going ashore and hit your head and drown. You can sail too close to the shore and get caught in the undertow. You can stay too far away from the shore and end up in Estonia in the fog. In the end you go aground and then everything really gets into a pickle. Although he thinks all the time about the things that might go wrong, Daddy loves great waves, particularly if they come from the south-west and get bigger and bigger.

Things turn out just as he said and the wind gets stronger and stronger. So now he doesn't need to be uneasy any longer but can be calm and cheerful while the wind blows.

Alas and alack we're leaving the shore Oh maiden so fair we'll see you no more. We're living under the spritsail on Acre Island and the wind is getting stronger all the time.

The Hermansons and the Seaforths arrived a little later. They have no children. They put up their sail for the night next to ours. And there we all were in the storm. All the females rushed around putting things straight and all the men rolled huge stones and shouted to each other and pulled the boats higher up. When the evening came Mummy

wrapped me in a blanket. From under the sail one could see a triangle of heather and surf and the sky that got bigger or smaller as the sail flapped in the wind. All night the men went down to the shore to see that everything was as it should be. They pulled up the boats and measured the height of the water and estimated the strength of the wind out on the point. From time to time Daddy came in to see whether we were still there and stuffed his pockets full of bread. He looked at me and knew that I was enjoying the storm just as much as he was.

Next morning we discovered a motorboat on the far side of the island. It lay there quite abandoned bumping up against the rocks; two planks had split and it was half full of water. And they had had no oars with them. They hadn't even risked their lives trying to save the boat.

It's just as I have always said, you can never rely on a motor, it just breaks down. People who go out to sea might well bother themselves to learn something about it first. They have never seen a spritsail in their lives and go and buy boats with high gunnels and then leave them lying on the beach without any tar and so they get leaky and become a disgrace to the whole community.

We stood looking at the boat for a while and then went straight up the shore and looked in the clump of willows behind the rocks on the beach, and there it all was – two-gallon canisters like a silver carpet under the bushes as far as you could see and a little higher up they had tucked the brandy under some spruce trees. Well, Daddy said. Well! It can't be true!

All the men started to run all over the place and the females followed with Mummy and me last, running as fast as we could.

On the lee-side Daddy and Mr Hermanson were talking to three soaking-wet fellows who were eating our sandwiches. The females and Mr Seaforth were standing a little way away. Then daddy came up to us and said, now this is what we're going to do. Hermanson and I will take them home because they have been drifting for three days without food and can hardly stand on their feet. If all goes well, each family will get four bottles and three canisters. Seaforth can't go with us as a matter of principle because he's a customs man himself.

We sat in a row and watched them sail away. Sometimes you could get a glimpse of the boat but sometimes you couldn't see them at all.

Mrs Seaforth looked at Mr Seaforth and said: think carefully what you're doing.

I'm thinking all right! He answered. Do you think this is easy for me? But I've made up my mind. I shan't take any notice of the whole thing, and I shan't accept a single bottle or a canister either. In any case, I'm on holiday and I'm not the only one who's taking them home. And they've eaten my sandwiches, too. Jansson would understand what I mean.

When daddy and Mr Hermanson came back they were soaked to the skin and very cheerful and immediately they came ashore they went to fetch the canisters. They took one each but Seaforth didn't take one at all because he was being loyal to the coastguards.

But they promised us four, said Mrs Hermanson. And three bottles of brandy.

That was while they were scared, said Daddy. When we got them home they changed their minds and said one canister for each family.

That's three then, said Mrs Hermanson. And we can share the Seaforth's.

That wouldn't be right, said Daddy. There are principles involved in this. Two canisters, and that's all. Besides, the journey itself was worth something. Women don't understand these things.

We hid the canisters in the seaweed.

Towards evening the wind died down and we sailed home, each family going their own way. Then we put the canisters in the fish-cage. We said nothing, we kept quiet.

There are people who sell canisters that they have found and overcharge for them. That's no way to behave. Others row the canisters to the coast-guard. It happened once in Pernby.

To buy a canister is like cheating the government, and anyway is too expensive, and one doesn't do that sort of thing. The only proper way is to find a canister and preferably save it at the risk of one's life. Such a canister is a source of satisfaction and does no harm to anybody's principles.

But a boat that has floated ashore or is just drifting is an entirely different matter. Boats are serious things. One has to search and search until one finds the owner even if it takes years to find him. It's just the same with fishing-nets that have broken loose and are drifting. They must go back to their owners. Everything else one is allowed to keep, logs, planks and pit-props and net-floats and buoys.

But the worst thing one can do is to take flotsam that has already been salvaged by someone else. That's unforgivable. If it has been piled up against a stone or collected in a neat pile with two stones on top of it, it is reserved. You can reserve it with two stones, but three are better. One stone is not to be relied on because it might have got there by accident. There are people who take other people's piles, or even worse just take the best things from each pile. I know! If one has rescued a plank one always recognises it again. And often one knows exactly who has been where one left it. But one says nothing about it afterwards because that would be in bad taste, and in any case who told one to reserve things with stones instead of making two trips to row everything home?

What is right and what is wrong is a very sensitive matter. One could say a lot about it; for example, if you come across a boat floating all by itself with a cabinet in it full of canisters, it goes without saying that one searches for the owner of the boat and keeps the cabinet oneself, if it is a nice one. But how many canisters is one allowed to keep? There's a lot of difference between a canister in a boat, in the undergrowth, or in the water or in a cabinet that is in a boat.

Once I found a boat made of bark that was called Darling. It was very beautifully made, with a hold, rudders, a wheelhouse and cloth sails. But Daddy said I didn't have to find out who owned it.

Maybe nothing is so important provided that it is small enough. At least that's what I think.

Albert

ALBERT IS ONE YEAR OLDER than I am, if you don't count six days.

For six days we are the same age.

He sat in the bay where the boats were and baited his father's long-line with bleak fish.

You must kill them first, I said. It's awful putting a hook in them while they're still alive.

Albert raised a shoulder slightly and I knew that it meant some kind of excuse and explanation: fish bite better if the bait is alive. He was wearing very faded overalls and a black cap that made his ears stick out.

How would you like to have a hook put through your back, I said. You'd be caught and you'd scream and try to get free and you'd just wait to be eaten up! What?

They don't scream, said Albert. It's always done like this.

You're cruel! I shouted. You do awful things. I don't want to talk to you any more!

He looked up at me a little sadly under his peaked cap and said: There, there! Then he went on putting the bleak on the line.

I walked away. At the boathouse I turned round and shouted: I'm just as old as you are! I'M JUST AS OLD AS YOU ARE!

Yes, I suppose you are, Albert replied.

I went and knocked nails into the raft but it wasn't any fun. Three nails went in crooked and I couldn't get them out again.

I went down to the beach again and said: fish suffer just as much as people do.

I don't think they do, said Albert. They're a lower form of life.

I said: how can you tell? Imagine if trees suffer as well! You saw them in half and they scream although you can't hear anything. Flowers scream when you pick them, though only a little bit.

Perhaps they do, said Albert. He said it in a very kind way but, even so, a little patronisingly and that made me angry again.

It was a nasty day. It was hazy and hot and sticky. I tried to cheer myself up by going to sit on the roof and sat there for a long time. I saw Albert and Old Charlie row out with the long-line. On the horizon there was a dirty-looking bank of clouds stretching all the way from Acre Island to Black Ball and the sea was completely smooth.

Then they came back and pulled up the boat.

After a while I could hear Albert knocking nails into the raft. I climbed down the ladder and went over to him and watched.

You knock nails in well, I said.

Then he hammered even more violently so that every nail went in with five blows. I began to feel better. I sat down in the grass and watched him and counted the hammer blows out loud. One nail went in with four. Then we both laughed.

Let's take it out straight away, I said. Now. We'll find a roller and get it into the sea at once.

We dragged up two planks and put a pit-prop across them and lifted the raft on to it. It was heavy and it creaked and bent a bit, but we got it up. Then all we had to do was roll it. The raft entered the water and glided out into the bay. It sat in the water beautifully. Albert went to fetch the paddles and we waded out, gave the raft a shove and jumped on. A little water came over the top but not much. We looked at each other and laughed.

It was slow work paddling but we got going. We reached deep water, but that was all right because we had both nearly learnt to swim. After a while we entered the sound near Red Rock.

Let's go to Sandy Island, I said.

I'm not so sure about that, Albert answered. It's going to get foggy.

But I paddled on and we moved slowly towards Sandy Island. We punted ourselves along the shore

and past the point. The sea was just as smooth and the bank of dirty clouds had grown and reached Egg Island. Albert pointed and said, that's fog. Now we're going home.

You aren't afraid of a little fog, are you? I asked. Let's go a little bit further and then we'll turn round.

I'm not so sure about that, said Albert.

You're not scared, are you? I said, and he paddled on and the raft went out to sea again. It was like moving across a black mirror, like standing on the sea, one could feel the faint swell all through one's body and one moved with it. The swell came from the south-east and rolled on towards Egg Island.

We're turning round now, said Albert firmly. The fog's coming.

It got cold very quickly and the fog was there, moving thickly around us, shutting us in on all sides. The smooth swell rolled out of the fog, crawled under the raft with a swallowing movement and rolled back into the fog the other side. I was freezing and was waiting for Albert to say, what did I say? Or, I told you so ... but he was silent and just paddled on and looked worried. He turned his head this way and that and listened and looked at the swell and kept in to the shore. After a while he kept more out to sea instead. Now there was a cross-wave in the swell and it started to come from all directions at the same time. Albert stopped paddling and said: we'd better wait until it lifts.

I was a little scared and said nothing at all.

If only Rosa would moo we'd get our direction, said Albert.

We listened in the fog but Rosa didn't moo, everything was as silent and deserted as the place where the world ends, and terribly cold.

Look, there's something floating, said Albert.

It was greyish-white and straggly and was moving very slowly in a circle towards us in the swell.

Albert said: it's a herring-gull. He poked it with the paddle and lifted it up onto the raft. It looked very big on the raft and went on shuffling round in a circle.

It's not well, I said. It's in pain.

Albert picked it up by the neck and looked at it, and it began to screech and flap one wing.

Let it go! I shouted. Everything looked so terrifying with the fog and the black water and the bird creeping around and screaming that I was beside myself and said: give it to me, I'll hold it in my lap, we must make it well again!

I sat down on the raft and Albert laid the bird in my lap and said: it won't get well. We must kill it.

You're always killing and killing, I said. Look how it's cuddling up to me, it's lonely and unhappy!

But Albert said it's got worms, and lifted up one wing and showed me that it was crawling with them. I screamed and threw the bird down. Then I started to cry and sat down and watched Albert pick up the bird very carefully and examine its wing.

There's nothing you can do about this, he explained. It's rotten. We'll have to kill it.

But let it fly away, I whispered. Perhaps it will get well after all.

Why should it suffer? said Albert. He took out his sheath-knife and held the bird by the head, pressing it down onto the raft. I stopped crying and watched, I just couldn't look away. Albert turned round so that he was between me and the gull. Then he cut right through its neck and let the head and the body of the gull slip into the water. When he turned round again he was as white as a sheet.

Look, there's blood! I whispered and began to tremble all over. Then he rinsed the blood away.

Don't get worked up about it, he said. You see, it was much the best way.

He was so kind that I began to cry again, and now it was lovely to be able to cry. Everything was over and everything was all right.

Albert always put things right. Whatever happened and however one behaved it was always Albert who put things right.

He stood looking at me, worried and not understanding. Don't be cross any longer, he said. Look, the fog's lifting and the wind is changing.

High Water

ONE SUMMER THE BOATHOUSE was empty because Old Charlie was out fishing all the time. Mummy sat on our veranda and drew illustrations and sent them to town with the herring boat. From time to time she took a dip in the sea and then she went on drawing again.

Daddy looked at her and then he went and looked in the boathouse and in the end he went to town and fetched his modelling stand and box of clay, his armatures and his modelling tools. He turned the boathouse into a studio and everybody got interested in it and helped him. They tried to tidy up all Old Charlie's tools and wanted to clean the floor, but that they weren't allowed to do.

Daddy got cross and then they understood that for Daddy the boathouse was a sacred place and not to be disturbed in any way. Nobody went down the field near the beach and the boats had to tie up at the herring jetty.

It was a very hot summer and the wind never blew.

Mummy drew and drew and every time a drawing was cleaned up with a rubber she allowed herself to take a dip. I stood next to the table on the veranda and waited till she held up a drawing so that the Indian ink could dry faster and we both laughed because we were thinking what it was like in town when drawing was done at night and made you so tired that you felt sick. Then we ran down to the beach and jumped into the sea. When Old Charlie had people from town staying with him I had to wear my knickers in the water.

Daddy was working in his new studio. He went there after he'd been fishing and had his breakfast. Daddy loves to go fishing. He gets up at four in the morning and takes his fishing rod and goes and looks at the bleak fish in the bait box.

It was so hot in the bay that the bleak all died, and we put out the net almost every evening just off Sandy Island. We put a packet of crispbread for Daddy on the veranda every morning. He filled his pockets full and rowed out through the sound.

A mooring-stone is very important. One can look for hours without finding a really good one, as they have to be slightly oval and have a notch in the middle. In the morning Daddy goes fishing by himself. Nobody interferes with him and nobody says he mustn't. The lighting is wonderful then and the rocks look just as good as if Cavvy had

painted them. One just sits and looks at the float, and one knows the fish will bite and when they'll bite. There's a rock underneath the water that has been named after Daddy, it's called Jansson's rock and will be called that for ever and ever. Then one makes one's way home slowly, looking to see if there's smoke coming out of the chimney.

Nobody else likes fishing. But Mummy helps with the bag-net and sits at the helm and trails a trolling-spoon. She has no sense of where the right spots are, but that's something people are born with and it's seldom found in women.

Daddy went to his new studio after breakfast. It was just as hot every day and there was never any wind.

Daddy got more and more glum. He began to talk politics. Nobody went near the boathouse and we didn't bathe near there either but went to the first bay instead.

The worst thing was the way in which Old Charlie's visitors behaved. They went out of their way to cut Daddy off when they saw him coming and addressed him as sculptor and asked him whether he had had any inspiration or not. I have never heard anything so tactless. They crept past the boathouse in an obvious way, putting their fingers up to their lips, whispering and nodding to one another and giggling, and naturally Daddy could see the whole performance through the window.

And the worst thing was that they suggested motifs to him. Mummy and I felt so terribly embarrassed for them, but what could we do?

Daddy became more and more glum and in the end he didn't speak to anyone at all. One morning he didn't even go fishing but stayed in bed staring at the ceiling with his lips pursed.

And it got hotter and hotter.

Then all of a sudden the water began to rise. We didn't notice it until the wind got up during the night. It all happened in half an hour. A mass of dry twigs and rubbish from the yard was blown against the window-panes and the storm roared through the forest, and it was so hot that one couldn't even bear to have a sheet over one in bed. The door was burst open and we ran out onto the steps and saw that there were white horses behind Red Rock, and then we saw the water glistening right up round the well and Daddy cheered up and shouted, well, I'll be damned! What weather! and put his trousers on and was outside in a jiffy. Old Charlie's visitors had been blown out onto the slope in their nightshirts and stood there all huddled together and had no idea at all what to do. But Mummy and Daddy went down to the beach and watched the jetty floating away towards Reed Island with all the boats pushing and nudging each other as though they were alive, and the fish-cage had broken adrift and all the pit-props were floating out through the sound. It was marvellous!

The grass was under water, the sea was rising all the time, and the storm and the night made the whole landscape look quite different.

Old Charlie ran to fetch the clothesline and Fanny stood there shouting and banging a tin can and her white hair was flying in all directions. Daddy rowed out to the jetty with a line and Mummy stood on the shore holding it.

Everything lying on the slope below the house had floated out to sea and the off-shore wind was carrying it out towards the sound and the wind was getting stronger and stronger and the water was rising higher and higher. I was shouting with glee, too, as I waded up and down and felt the floating grass getting tangled round my legs. I was trying to save planks and from time to time Daddy ran past hauling logs and shouting: what do you think of this! The wind's getting stronger all the time! He flung a rope to the visitors and shouted: take hold of this, damn you! We must get the jetty up into the field! Do something! Don't just stand there!

And the visitors hauled on the rope and were soaked to the skin in their nightshirts and had no idea what fun the whole thing was, which served them right.

In the end we saved everything that could be saved and Mummy went into the house to make tea. I pulled off my clothes and was wrapped in a blanket and sat and watched Mummy lighting the fire. The window-panes rattled and were quite dark and it started to rain.

Then Daddy burst in and went into the kitchen and shouted: Damn it! Can you imagine what's happened! The water has risen nearly two feet in the boathouse! The clay looks like porridge. It's a damned nuisance, but there's nothing to be done about it!

How terrible, said Mummy, looking just as pleased as Daddy.

I've been down to the first bay, Daddy said, and it's blowing hard down there and a whole load of logs is floating in. I've no time for tea now. I'll be back later.

All right, said Mummy. I'll keep it warm.

Then Daddy went out again. Mummy poured out tea for us all. It was the best storm we had ever had.

Jeremiah

ONE YEAR TOWARDS AUTUMN a geologist was living in the pilot's hut. He couldn't speak either Finnish or Swedish, he just smiled and flashed his black eyes. He would look at people and immediately make them feel how surprised and happy he was to meet them at last and then he just walked on with his hammer and hammered a rock here and there. His name was Jeremiah.

He borrowed a boat to row out to the islands and Old Charlie stood and sniggered at Jeremiah because he rowed so miserably. One felt embarrassed for Jeremiah when he took to the water and Daddy wondered what the pilots thought when they saw him rowing.

Jeremiah and I were together every day. We walked around the bays and I was allowed to carry his little box while he hammered away at the rocks. Sometimes I was allowed to stand guard over the boat.

It was very sensible of me to look after Jeremiah. He couldn't even tie a proper half-hitch – when he tried to it looked more like some kind of bow. Sometimes he even forgot to tie the boat up. But it was because he didn't care about anything else in the world except stones. They didn't have to be pretty and round or odd in any way. He had ideas of his own about stones and they were quite different from anybody else's.

I never got in his way and I only showed him my collection of stones once. Then he put on such a great show of admiring them that I was embarrassed. He overdid things in the wrong way. But later on he learned better.

We walked along the beach, him in front and me behind. When he stopped, I stopped and stood still and watched while he hammered away, but I never came too close. He hadn't often got time for me. But sometimes when he turned round and caught sight of me he pretended to be terribly surprised. He bent forward and screwed up his eyes and tried to look at me through his magnifying glass, then shook his head as though it was impossible that anyone could be as tiny as I was. Then he saw me anyway and stepped backwards in surprise and pretended that he was holding something very very small in his hands and we both started to laugh.

Sometimes he would draw both of us in the sand, one very tall and one very small, and once

I was allowed to borrow his jersey when the wind got up. But otherwise he mostly hammered away at the rocks and forgot all about me. I didn't mind. I always walked behind him and in the morning I waited outside the pilots' hut until he woke up.

We played a game. I put a present on his doorstep and then hid myself and when he came out he found the present and was delighted. He puzzled over it and scratched his head and threw his arms in the air and then began to look for me. He looked in a rather stupid way but that was all part of the game. He had to take a long time to find me and to discover how terribly tiny I was. I tried to make myself smaller and smaller so that he would be delighted. We hammered away at the rocks for many days together. Then it got cloudy and windy and rather cold, and then she came.

She had the same kind of hammer as Jeremiah and walked around hammering in exactly the same way as he did and she couldn't speak Swedish or Finnish either. She lived in Old Charlie's sauna.

I knew that Jeremiah wanted to hammer on his own. He didn't want her to come with him but she just came. If one wants to collect stones one should be allowed to do so on one's own. She could have looked for them on her own, but she didn't. She kept appearing from a different direction and always pretended to be surprised at meeting Jeremiah. But her game of pretending was phoney and hadn't anything to do with us two.

I followed behind with Jeremiah's little box and stood waiting while he hammered away. I made sure that the boat was properly tied up. But of course we couldn't play our game of how tiny I was while she was there.

In the beginning she smiled at me, but in fact all she did was bare her teeth. I stared at her until she looked away and went on hammering. I followed them and stood waiting and every time she turned round she looked at me and I never looked back at her. We froze because the wind blew right in our faces and the sun never shone. I could see that she was freezing cold and that she was afraid of the water. But she came in the boat too and she never let him go out to the islands by himself.

She sat in the stern and gripped the gunnels with both hands and I could see from them how scared she was. She pressed her knees tightly together and craned her neck and gulped. She didn't look at the waves but just stared at Jeremiah the whole time and he rowed zigzag as best he could against the wind and off they went together and got smaller and smaller.

I wasn't allowed to go with them in the boat any longer. They pretended that it was too small. It was a stout flat-bottomed boat and I could well have sat in the bows. Jeremiah knew it but he was afraid of her. I waited until I saw them set off and then come back to the bays. Then I would hide in the shelter of a rock and watch them and wherever they came ashore I was there to meet them and tie up their boat.

I knew that nothing was fun any longer and couldn't be, but I followed them all the same. I couldn't stop following them, every day and all day until evening, and I had my own food with me. But we didn't swap sandwiches any more. We kept ourselves to ourselves and we all sat at the same distance from each other and none of us said anything.

Then we would get up and walk along the shore. Once she stopped and stood still and waited for me without turning round. I stopped too because her back took on a dangerous shape. And then she turned round and said something to me. It was the first time she had opened her mouth. At first I didn't understand. Then she said it again, over and over, very loud and in a shrill voice, go home! Go home, go home! Somebody had taught her to say go home but it sounded queer.

I looked down at my feet and waited until she went on, and then I followed again.

But in the morning she wasn't there. So I put my present on the steps of the pilot's hut and hid. I could stay in hiding as long as they liked. Then Jeremiah came out onto the steps and found the present and was surprised. He began to search for me and I was terribly tiny, so tiny that I could have fitted into his pocket.

But gradually everything changed. I grew and he found me much too quickly. He wasn't at all surprised. At last the awful thing had happened: we were playing the game because we had started to play it and thought it was somehow too embarrassing to stop.

One morning Jeremiah came out onto the steps and found his present. He threw his arms into the air as usual and clutched his head. But then he didn't take his hands away but held his head far too long. Then he came right up to the pine tree where I was hiding and stood in front of me and smiled and I could see he was baring his teeth just like she did and wasn't at all friendly. It was so awful that I just ran away.

I was ashamed for both our sakes all day. At three o'clock the sun came out and I went back to the bays.

They were in the third bay. He sat hammering and she was looking on a little way away. She wasn't cold any longer and had taken off her woolly cap and undone her hair – masses of it that fell all over the place while she was looking at him. Then she went closer and laughed and bent down to see what he was doing and her hair fell all over him and he got scared and straightened up and bumped her nose. I think it was her nose. She nearly fell over so Jeremiah took a firm hold of her and for an instant they looked like paper dolls. Then she began to speak very rapidly and Jeremiah held on to her and listened.

He was so far away from me that I had to shout so that he would hear me and I shouted for all I was worth. But he just walked away and she was left standing there staring at me and I stared back. I stared and stared at her until I had stared her into little pieces and I thought, you're big and scraggy like a carthorse and nobody can hunt for you in the grass and you couldn't hide anywhere because you can be seen the whole time and you can't surprise anybody and make them feel good! You have completely spoilt our game for no reason at all because you can't play games yourself! O alas and alack! No one wants your presents. He doesn't want them. You're nobody's surprise, and you can't understand because you're not an artist! And so I went a little closer and humiliated her by saying the most terrible thing of all: amateur! You're an amateur! You're not a real artist!

She stepped backwards and screwed up her face. Then I daren't look at her any longer because it's an awful shame to see a grown-up person cry. So I looked at the ground and waited a long time. I heard her walk away. When I looked up she had gone.

Jeremiah was on the point hammering away. So I went back to the pilots' hut and took back my present. It was a very beautiful skeleton of a bird, and quite white. Mummy gave me a box just the right size and I took the skeleton with me when I went back to town. It's very unusual to come across the skeleton of a bird which is the right chalky-white colour.

Dressing Up

NOBODY ELSE BUT FANNY was allowed to light the fire in the sauna on Saturdays. It was the only job she really liked. She marched up and down in front of the house all day on her spindly legs, which were as white as her hair, carrying wood, very slowly and only two logs at a time. On Saturdays Fanny was the most important person in the whole place and therefore she sang to herself, monotonously and shrilly.

Then they pulled the sauna down. Only the stove and the bench and the doorposts were left standing in the rain. Summer was over and Mummy had gone back to town. Daddy was out fishing and I was walking around in the rain. It rained and rained. The field was brown and waterlogged and smelt rotten and the logs of the sauna walls were lying all over the place because the ants had eaten them from the inside and they weren't worth saving.

When Saturday came round again Fanny carried wood down to the sauna and filled the stove.

She stood and stared at the bench and the empty doorway and muttered to herself. Her wrinkled face was quite expressionless and her eyes too. I could see the rain running down her wrinkles in little rivulets. She removed some faded leaves from the bench, muttering to herself the whole time. Then she stood and waited until the next leaf floated down and removed that too. Finally she sat on the bench next to the cat. They looked as though they were at the theatre.

I went into the kitchen and lay down on the woodbox and listened to the rain until I fell asleep. When I woke up it had stopped raining. I took the big red tablecloth and went down to the sauna. Daddy was still out fishing. Fanny was still sitting on the bench but the cat had disappeared.

I climbed on to a bucket and threw the tablecloth over the door-frame so that it hung almost to the ground. It looked much redder out of doors.

That's the curtain, I said.

Fanny cackled but said nothing.

I went into the house to fetch the gong and hung it on a nail beside the curtain. Then I carried out all the lanterns and lamps and candlesticks and put them round the stage. Fanny followed everything I did very closely. It was dripping everywhere but it wasn't actually raining. The clouds were so heavy that it was almost dusk.

When everything was ready I dressed up as Princess Florinna. I put on Mummy's bright pink petticoat and the cat's Sunday bow and tied a green scarf round my tummy.

When I got back Fanny had picked lots of apples and arranged them in a circle round the theatre – they were so yellow that the ground around them looked almost black. An even darker cloud appeared so I lit the lights. It was difficult to get the lamps to burn, but I managed it in the end. But the lanterns wouldn't work at all.

The cat jumped up beside Fanny and I gave them each a programme and put one in the place reserved for Daddy.

Then I went behind the curtain and struck the gong. I pulled back the curtain and entered the stage. I started by bowing to Fanny and then to the cat and they gazed at me very intently.

I cried: Oh! come sweet blue-bird mine on speedy wing, oh come and make my heart once more to sing! I wrung my hands and ran up and down because I was shut up in a tower and waiting for Prince Amundus.

Then I was Holofernes and pushed out my tummy and bellowed: Says she so, the waspish creature? Devil take me, I'll soon teach her!

It began to rain again. Out by Red Rock Daddy was on his way home again. There was a narrow yellow streak in the sky behind Sandy Island. The rain put all the candles out but the lamps went on burning. Suddenly I was the wicked queen and shouted: What see I here? You now my eyes appall, Oh wretched creature vanish from my ball! Aside. At sight of her with wrath my blood doth flame.

I was Florinna and answered timidly: My Queen, oh hear me, I am not to blame!

It rained harder and harder. The cat began to wash herself. So I went straight into the scene where Amundus is put under a spell. Circe, black and menacing, crept behind the stove and said: Arigida rigida igida gida! Miraho! Iraho! Aho! Amundus! Mundus! Undus! Ndus! Dus! Us! S! She flung open the door of the stove with a hiss.

Then Fanny stood up and started to stamp, shouting Oh! Oh! Oh!

Amundus said: Unhand me wicked queen as black as night!

And the Queen said: Florinna now you would abandon quite?

Oh! Oh! Oh! screamed Fanny.

Owls fly and little pixies trip over the stage. I was Florinna again. But before I could say a single word, Fanny got off the bench and came on to the stage and started clapping her hands together and crying Oh! Oh! Oh!

Clear off! I said angrily. It's not finished. You're not supposed to clap yet!

But Fanny didn't take any notice of me. She crouched down in front of the stove and got some birch-bark to light. All the smoke came out of the top of the stove as there wasn't any chimney left and the stove was wet anyway. She went on stamping round and started to sing her Great Rain Song.

You silly ass! I shouted. You're the audience!

Daddy came across the field. He stopped and said: what on earth are you doing? He looked very surprised.

I'm acting! I shouted. It was for you as well! And now Fanny has ruined the whole thing!

The rain was pouring down now and all the lamps had gone out. I started to cry as hard as I could.

Never mind, Daddy said. Calm down now. He didn't really know what to say. After a while he said: I've caught a four-pounder.

Oh! Oh! Oh! cried Fanny.

I went on ahead to the house, crying all the way, but now it was mostly to make an impression. Daddy followed and lit a candle because all the lamps were in the theatre. He showed me the pike he had caught.

It's a lovely one, I said, because one must always say something when someone catches a fish. And then it was too late to cry any more. I put on my ordinary clothes again and we had a cup of tea together.

All the time we could hear Fanny beating the gong and singing her rain song. The whole field was full of smoke. Soon the cat got tired of it all and came in too.

That's Circe, I said casually. She was turned into a cat.

What did you say? Daddy asked.

Oh nothing, I said, because it didn't seem important any longer.

Next day Fanny was in very good spirits. The sauna door had fallen over and the curtain lay in the grass. We spread it out on the veranda table to dry and left it here until the following summer.

Pets and Females

DADDY LOVES ALL ANIMALS because they don't contradict him. He likes ones that are furry best. And they love him, too, because they know that they can do just as they like.

But it's quite a different matter with Females.

If you make statues of them they become women but as long as they remain Females things are difficult. They can't even pose properly and they talk much too much. Mummy isn't a Female of course, and never has been one.

Once at twilight when Daddy was standing outside the house a bat flew straight into his arms. Daddy stood quite still and it crept inside his jacket and hung upside down and went to sleep. Daddy didn't move. We carried his dinner outside to him and he ate it very carefully. No one was allowed to speak. Then we took his plate away and Daddy stayed where he was until it got dark. Then the bat flew around for a while and came back to him again.

This time it only stopped for a moment – a kind of courtesy call.

The summer when Mummy made porridge or spaghetti for Pellura every day we didn't catch any fish in the nets at all. Daddy went out on to the rock and called: Pellura, Pellura, and the gull came to him. Sometimes it brought its children along.

There was a Female who maintained that Pellura wasn't a common gull at all but a herring-gull that ate up baby eiders and Daddy just hated that Female until she went away.

Pellura had flesh-pink legs and was actually a herring-gull and did eat baby eiders but after the Female had gone we still believed that he was a common gull.

He came when Daddy called, and you can never be taken in by a pet and you can never fool it either. It's more difficult in town but we do our best. Last spring we had nineteen canaries. I must tell you, once and for all, that canaries are very virulent birds.

It starts with the mother bird and the father bird. They have babies. And before the babies get a single feather on their bodies they have to leave home and the father bird sings again and the mother bird lays new eggs. That's how things go with canaries.

Daddy had a lot of trouble with them. They perched on the indoor aerial, singing and flapping their wings and splashing about and everything was calm and peaceful and all of a sudden they started being rotten to each other and attacked the smallest and ugliest of them and plucked him bald.

Then Daddy tapped them on the head with his modelling stick and said: you little devils, and they calmed down and just sang.

Daddy went up to his modelling stand and put on some more clay and then stepped backwards again. The rabbits lolloped forward, one on each side of him, and back again. They never changed sides. They loved him. But sometimes it became too much for them and they fought behind his back because they were jealous of each other. Then Daddy tapped them on the head with his modelling stick. Sometimes he tapped me on the head.

But he never taps Poppolino. After Mummy, Daddy loves Poppolino better than anything in the world. Poppolino is even allowed to jump through today's newspaper because he's Daddy's friend. He lives in a big cage on Daddy's bunk but as soon as he hangs upside down by his tail he's allowed to come out.

They sit in front of the wireless together and Poppolino listens with one of the headphones and turns the knobs to find the crackling noises. Or else they go to the shop and buy herrings.

When Daddy goes to the shop he often has to tap Females on the head because they can never make up their minds and finger the food and talk politics in a silly way.

And he has to do the same thing every time we go to the cinema because they don't take their hats off. Females are difficult.

The fact is that on the whole they are asocial and wouldn't even obey orders during a war, but in any case they're scared when Daddy taps them on the head, which is always a good thing.

Mummy is no Female and she always takes her hat off.

Mummy looks at Daddy and says: yes, perhaps you're right, and when she's alone she does things her own way.

Once Daddy wanted to take Poppolino to see a jungle film but they weren't allowed in. Daddy is always having trouble with Poppolino. If it's not Females it's Poppolino.

On another occasion they went to Gambrini's Restaurant together to have a nice evening out and were sent home before eleven o'clock. Poppolino hadn't exactly behaved badly, just shown a little too much interest in a hat, which was the wrong colour anyway. Pets *do* complicate life.

Many times it happened that Poppolino ate up one of the canaries and each time Daddy was just as sad. But when he thought about it afterwards he realised that it was a good thing after all because there were far too many canaries anyway. Things even themselves out in nature. Anyway, they did their business all over Mummy's drawings, and – even worse – in her hair!

I know that Daddy adores Mummy's beautiful hair just as much as James Oliver Curwood adored Jeanette's hair in Alaska. He put his nose in it in front of the fire and sang softly together with his faithful dogs. Or perhaps he was just whimpering. James Oliver Curwood, I mean, not Daddy.

Daddy always talks about Mummy's hair when he's having a party and he goes on to talk about the sort of hair he doesn't like. There are Females who walk in the street with their hair hanging all over the place, even falling in their eyes. And they never wash it. Females of that kind have no natural dignity and know nothing about their role in society.

The saddest thing that can happen to a man is when his hair gets thin on top. It shows that his hat is too small and means that he is bourgeois and probably henpecked.

But to be bald is something quite different, that is if the skull is sculptural and preferably dolicho-cephalic like Cavvy's.

But Daddy has most trouble with Females, particularly if they are posing for him. They often have ugly knees although the torso is good and more often than not they have very tiresome toes. Daddy doesn't like modelling toes and wants Mummy to do it for him. But Mummy can't be bothered with toes either.

Poppolino has very pretty toes and fingers. He puts his arms round Daddy's neck and screams with affection. He comforts anyone who cries. When he gets loose in the street and climbs up the wall of a house the only way of getting him down again is to sit on the pavement and burst into tears.

Silly children come up to Daddy and ask him if he's sitting crying because the monkey has bitten him. What an idea! Poppolino is always biting Daddy but Daddy never cries and he's never angry with Poppolino because they are such great friends.

Although they were eaten, the canaries multiplied until there were twenty-four of them. Then Mummy and Daddy put an advertisement in the paper which said that anyone could get a canary for nothing if they came to our house.

Females started to arrive at half-past seven in the morning and they went on coming all day until dark.

One Female had her own motor-car and another had her own servant who carried the bird-cage for her and they all said that we had terrible stairs and told us all about the canaries they had owned earlier, the ones that had died and the ones that had flown away. Some of the Females burst into tears and Daddy ran around catching canaries for them and when there weren't any more left then the Females were given an egg wrapped in cotton wool to take home, and when the eggs were finished they just came in and burst into tears.

Poppolino rattled his cage and didn't feel sorry for the Females because he could see that they were only crying because they liked crying.

No work got done that day and afterwards the whole place was very quiet and we regretted having got rid of the canaries.

But Mousey was still in his box. Mousey was Daddy's friend in a quiet almost secretive way. The box was full of turf and had a wall of glass. Behind the glass you could see an underground tunnel which Mousey had dug. But he hardly ever came out himself.

Daddy stood outside the box and waited and tapped with his modelling stick and said: come to Daddy little sweety. After a while a quivering little nose appeared out of the tunnel but never more than the nose. Then Daddy was happy and went back to work. When one is working it's a good idea sometimes to take an interest in something that's friendly but doesn't talk.

We shouldn't have let a charwoman into the studio, and we never shall again. She took a fistful of cotton waste and rubbed the glass and then threw the cotton waste into the box. Mousey didn't like the glass being cleaned and never showed his nose again. But he liked the cotton waste and made himself a nest out of it which none of us ever saw.

Daddy got depressed about it. For a time he threw fish out of the bedroom window to the gulls instead but it didn't feel as nice and could never be the same after Pellura. Anyway, the police came and made a fuss. We never understood why.

Daddy has had trouble with pets all his life. Take Midge for example, who died of food poisoning. Granny found him in a dustbin during the 1918 war. His tail had been cut off and he looked awful. He was so tiny and ghastly and everybody who saw him was upset and wanted to get rid of him as quickly as possible. That was why Granny was given some beef stew for Midge whenever she took him to the kitchen door of a restaurant, which meant that the family had something to eat every day.

Daddy and Mummy always tell the story of Midge, sometimes several times over to the same people. Sometimes they say that Midge got some of the stew and sometimes they say that he didn't get any at all. I never tell the same story over again to the same person.

All dogs are loyal. They remind one a lot of men, with the exception perhaps of pug-dogs. There's something wrong about having a pug-dog. If a Female has a pug-dog you know at once that she's on the shelf. This happened particularly when Daddy was young. But it isn't a good thing to get married and desert the pug-dog, either. Many have done that and gone from the frying-pan into the fire, Daddy says. Even if one has a pug-dog, one must be loyal. It's all *very* difficult.

Actually, things are difficult for me, too. I don't think about Females very much because they only drive you out of your mind if you are a sculptor. But I think about Daddy's pets all the time. There have been so many of them that it has been difficult to keep count of them all and there's always the same trouble with them whether they are furry or not. I get so tired thinking about them.

Poppolino is Daddy's friend once and for all just as much as Cavvy is. It's a fact and Mummy and I can't do anything about it. He'll live until he's a hundred years old.

But all the others! The sheep, for example. It walked on to the veranda without wiping its feet first. It stamped and banged around and got everything it took a fancy to. Then it took itself off again on its stiff legs and with its silly bleating and its silly dirty backside wobbling as it went down the steps and it had no idea of all the love that it had been given!

Cats! They didn't understand either. They were either podgy puddings that just slept or they were beautiful and wild and took no notice of Daddy at all.

And the squirrels! He was never allowed to stroke them. They snapped and were quick and independent. They just wanted to grab and grab and grab and then jump away and look pretty in peace and quiet on their own.

But I tell you that the worst of all was the crow. My goodness, that crow was artful! She knew all about Daddy and she liked being stroked. She was much more dangerous than Poppolino. Poppolino lives by his feelings and can't tell the difference between right and wrong.

But the crow knew. She worked things out and was calculating. She looked at Daddy and then she looked at me. You could see that she was sizing things up carefully. Then she croaked in a very deep voice, plaintively and tenderly and hung her head and went up to Daddy's legs. She rubbed herself against him, gently and helplessly, because she knew that that was what he liked.

But when she was alone with me she said caw! caw! suddenly and shamelessly, like the crow she was, and we stared at each other and never became reconciled, and I knew that she had fleas!

Daddy never saw them because he didn't want to. He let her croak and gurgle in her usual simpering way and said: now listen, do you know it's three o'clock in the morning? Do you imagine I've got something here for you? Do you think I've got time to bother with every little crow?

You have, you have, you have, I lay in bed and thought, biting the sheets and hating the crow. Of course you've got time and you worked out last night what you were going to give her to eat. Then they went out to have a look.

One day she was sitting on the railing by the steps picking and plucking herself. Caw! caw! said Daddy enticingly from the veranda, but the crow just went on picking for fleas.

Can't you hear him calling? I said, and pushed her and she got her leg caught in the railings and it snapped in two. Crows' legs are very thin.

Human beings don't realise how thin they can be. She flapped her wings and screeched, but this time she was screeching naturally and not just to attract Daddy's attention.

Then she died and was buried. Daddy said nothing. I went and sat behind the cellar and worked out a funeral elegy. It went like this: Ah! little crow, how short was your life! Over for you is all trouble and strife! There in your breast struck the life-taking shot, Ending for ever your terrestrial lot. Now you may sit on some far-distant star, White as a swan – oh! I pray that you are! Sunset now glows, the horizon's all gold, Eider and swallow her rays bright enfold, Bullfinch and eagle, but not little crow – silent she lies in her grave here below! See where the full moon looks down from on high, Peaceful and calm on the spot where you lie!

I heard Daddy say to Mummy that it was a talented bit of poetry. Perhaps my poem has helped him to grieve less. If it hasn't, then the crow's ghost will haunt me until I die. Who cares, anyway? I was the one who won!

And another thing. Daddy doesn't love flies. Is there such a big difference between crows and flies? Both fly. Both are greyish-black. Both have children, flies quite obviously. They sit on top of each other and carry on just like the canaries and make lots and lots of babies all the time. But Daddy doesn't like them and just wants to kill them. He catches them in a net and when the net is full and there are about six million innocent flies in it crawling around and crying for help he ties the top of the bag and drops it into boiling water. How *can* he!

I walk two miles as far as the village before I let the flies out. Otherwise they would be drowned in boiling water. I wonder whether they like flies in the village? I'm the only one who takes pity on them and no one will help me save them. I asked Alan, who is a temporary visitor for the summer. Don't be silly, he said. You know that I only bother about animals after they're dead. I bury them.

Well, I said, how about flies when they are dead? Do you put each of them in a separate grave or all in the same one? But he just stared at me and said again: you're silly.

Alan has five graveyards full of crosses and he collects corpses all day long and everybody is fed up with him.

The only person who helps him is Fanny. She's good at finding corpses and lines them up on the steps every morning. A row of pretty pebbles, a row of shells and a row of corpses.

Alan doesn't dare learn to swim and he can't play games. He'll be going away soon, which is a jolly good thing. A funeral is interesting every now and then, but not the whole time.

In any case I shall visit his graveyards sometimes in the evening and sing a hymn or recite my funeral elegy; one should always maintain tradition, Daddy says.

The Spinster Who
Had An Idea

WEEK AFTER WEEK SHE SAT making steps with cement outside Old Charlie's little house. But it was very slow work. They had to be terribly pretty and unlike any other steps in the whole world. They were to be her present to us for being allowed to live in our attic.

She woke up earlier and earlier in the morning. We heard her squeaking terribly slowly down the stairs because she was so afraid of waking us up. Then she started moving her buckets and her stones outside the veranda just as slowly, and occasionally we heard a little clanking sound and then a scraping noise and a thud and a splash and in the end we were wide awake and lay waiting for the next cautious movement.

Sometimes she creaked across the veranda to fetch something she had forgotten and opened the door, put her fingers to her lips and whispered: sleep soundly, ssh! Don't worry about me. And then she smiled sadly and secretively. She was tall and thin and had anxious eyes set close together and she had reached that certain age. What exactly that certain age was and why she had reached it, no one would tell me, but in any case life wasn't easy for her and the steps were all she cared about. That's why we admired what she was doing so much.

When we came out on the veranda she shouted No! no! no! no! wait a moment! She jumped to her feet quickly and began to haul up a plank and lifted one end of it onto the threshold and the other end onto a box. While we were balancing ourselves on the plank she looked terrified and implored: I've only just cemented it! Do be careful and please don't tread anywhere near it!

Then Daddy picked up the plank so she could go on cementing and she thanked him much too profusely for his help.

Day after day she was on her knees trying to fit stones into the cement and round her she had buckets of cement and water, and sand and rags and trowels and small sticks and spades. The stones had to be flat and smooth and pretty in colour. They lay there arranged in piles according to a very well thought-out plan and on no account were they to get mixed up. The smallest stones were red and white and were kept separately in a box.

She cemented and thought and then worked away and made a mistake and then thought again and sometimes she just sat and stared at the whole thing.

We started to get out through the bedroom window, but only when she wasn't looking. Once when Mummy was carrying some pails of water over the plank, she spilled a few drops and a very important part of the concrete was spoiled. Then we started lifting the pails of water through the window too.

I knew that I wasn't allowed to help her because she wanted to play on her own. So I just stood and looked on.

She had begun with the small red and white stones and was poking a long row of them into the cement. It was supposed to be some kind of saying, and every time a little stone got into the wrong place she gave a little wail.

Don't you like playing? I asked.

She didn't understand what I meant. It's so difficult, she said. You mustn't look! So I went away.

She had thought that she would put Bless All Those Who Cross This Threshold on the steps but she forgot to measure it. So when at last she got to the end there wasn't enough room for Threshold. Thresh was all that she could fit in.

You ought to have measured it before you started, Daddy said. And used a bit of string to keep it straight. I could have shown you how to do it.

It's easy to say that when it's too late! She cried. I don't think you care one bit about my steps! I know you climb in the window just to show me I'm in the way!

Dammit, what other way should we go with your pots and pans all over the place, Daddy said. Then she started to cry and rushed up to the attic. Daddy was left standing there looking miserable and said, oh damn!

The steps never really got finished. She lost interest in them and moved all her things down to the big rock instead in order to cement stones in the big tub. The plank was taken away. But the hole in the concrete where she had started to cry was still there staring at us.

All the next day she emptied the big tub with buckets. When she had almost reached the bottom she borrowed the scoop. Then she used a tea cup and a sponge. But right at the bottom there were nasty creepy-crawly things living in the slime and she was afraid of them although she felt sorry for them. It was so awful getting them up from the bottom she was on the point of screaming but she said, it's got to be done, and she carried them over to another tub and in between tea cups she put her arms in the sea and waved them about while her tears fell into the water.

When the tub was quite empty she started to put rows of stones at the bottom and then cemented them. She twisted and turned each stone in order to get it to fit but she couldn't do it. She tried one stone after another but none of them would fit. Then she noticed that I was standing by the wood-pile. You mustn't look! she shouted. So I went away again.

She looked for new stones in the bay, but they were either the wrong shape or the wrong colour. But the hardest thing was to get the stones clean when they were finally in place. She washed them and wiped them and rinsed her rag again and again but when the stone was dry it still had a little fleck of cement on it and then she had to start from the beginning again. And in the winter the tub froze at the bottom and the whole thing cracked. It was very difficult being a spinster.

When she came back the following summer I was terribly afraid that everything would go wrong for her again. We had filled the hole on the steps with sand and poured a little milk into the tub so that she wouldn't be able to see how awful the bottom looked. But she wasn't interested in cement any longer. She had brought with her a whole suitcase full of her scrapbooks with glossy cut-out pictures and she put them to soak in the washtub. Then she peeled off all the glossy pictures and laid them out to dry on the slope. It was a beautiful calm Sunday and the slope was dotted with pictures of roses and angels by the thousand and she was happy again and carried them up to her room in the attic. It was such a relief to see that she was happy!

Things seem to be a bit better this time, Mummy said.

But Daddy said: do you think so? I'm not so sure, but as usual I'm not saying anything.

And she started sticking boxes together. She sat in her room in the attic making little boxes with lots of little compartments which she covered with glossy pictures both on the inside and on the outside. The glossy pictures stuck straightaway and kept their colour and didn't have to fit because she stuck them on top of each other.

The room in the attic was full of paper and pots of paste and boxes and big piles of glossy pictures that one wasn't allowed to touch. She sat down in the middle of it all, sticking and sticking and in the end the pile of scrap paper reached up to her knees. But she never put anything in the boxes and never gave any of them away.

Are they always going to be empty? I asked.

She looked at the box she was making and didn't answer. Her long face had an anxious look and there was a glossy picture sticking to her fringe.

I got fed up with her because she wasn't happy. I don't like it when people find life difficult. It gives me a bad conscience and then I get angry and begin to feel that they might as well go somewhere else.

But Granny liked her because she had been a good customer at the button shop and they used to read Allers' *Family Magazine* together during the winter.

Granny had a lot of little boxes with lots of compart-ments but at least she put buttons in them. While Granny's button business was a glorious success each kind of button was kept separate but when the business went bust the buttons got into the wrong compartments, which was actually much more fun.

Before the police came to the shop Granny managed to rescue a lot of button boxes which she hid under her skirts just as she had hidden guns during the 1918 war. She also rescued tons of Allers' *Family Magazines* and little porcelain dogs and velvet pin cushions and a quantity of nightcaps and silk ribbons and then she sighed and said, bless me; now we shall have to draw crosses on the ceiling again! And she carried everything to Daddy's and Mummy's studio.

Mummy hid all the Allers' *Family Magazines* but Granny and I found them, particularly the ones with the whole-page pictures of sad things. A Young Witch Being Led to the Stake. A Heroine's Death.

And every copy of the magazine was kept for the spinster. Granny and she used to read them in secret in the bedroom.

Once she came to read Allers' *Family Magazine* on the worst possible day she could have picked. Daddy was busy making a plaster cast. And it was a particularly large and difficult one that had to be made in sections.

The plaster was already mixed so, as you know, it was a question of seconds. You mustn't touch it and you must hardly breathe. I should never have dreamed of going into the studio just then. Mummy and Daddy were standing ready with their plastering clothes on and the whole floor was covered with brown paper.

And just then she came in and said: hallo! hallo! Something's going on here, I can see. Don't let me disturb you!.

I was standing behind the curtains and watching. She went straight up to the tub of plaster and poked a finger in it and said, plaster! how funny, and just now when I'm particularly interested in plaster!

Mummy said: we're working. And Daddy looked ready to murder somebody. I was so frightened and embarrassed that I climbed up onto my bunk. I was sure that Daddy would throw clay at her because that's what he always does when he's angry. But the only thing I could hear was the soft slapping sound of wet plaster. They had started casting. She babbled away the whole time without realising that she was interrupting an almost sacred ceremony. Granny came out of the bedroom for a moment, looked terrified and went back inside.

After a while I ventured down. By that time she had got an overall on and was standing by the window with both hands in a little bowl of plaster.

Now it's going hard! She shouted. What shall I do next?

And instead of hitting her on the head, Daddy went up to her and showed her what to do. I looked at Mummy. She grinned and shrugged her shoulders.

The spinster had cut out a picture from Aller's *Family Magazine* and put it face down on a saucer.

Have you greased the saucer properly? Daddy asked severely.

Yes, yes, she said. Just as you said.

Well, pour it on, said Daddy. But don't put your finger in it.

She poured the plaster into the saucer and Daddy took the putty knife and made the whole thing even. Then he said: do you want a hook too?

Yes, yes, she whispered, and was so happy that she drew her breath as she spoke. It's to hang on the wall.

Daddy sniffed and went up to the reel of steel wire and cut off a bit. He made a loop and stuck it in the plaster on one side. Don't touch it, he said. Leave it to dry.

You *are* kind, she breathed and the tears came to her eyes. I shall come back tomorrow and bring my glossy cut-out pictures with me. They will be even more beautiful.

And she did, too!

All the time the plaster-casting was going on, she stood at the work-bench and put glossy cut-outs into a saucer and poured plaster on them and put a loop at one end just as Daddy had taught her to do. A whole row of plaster pictures lay on the bench, each with a big bright glossy cut-out in the middle. The pictures curved beautifully over the chalky-white plaster and had no spots on them at all because she got better and better at it all the time.

She was beside herself with joy. Granny came in and praised her. She gave each of us a picture and she hung Daddy's on the studio wall.

I didn't know what to think. The plaster pictures were really the most beautiful things I had ever seen, but they weren't Art. One couldn't respect them at all. Actually one should really have despised them. It was a terrible thing to do to make such pictures in Daddy's studio and, what's more, while a plaster cast was being made.

The worst thing was that she didn't even look at the statue standing there waiting to be touched up and given its patina, but just babbled on about her own pictures. The whole work-bench was full of them and looked like a cake-shop.

In the end she was given a big bag of plaster and all the pictures were packed up in a box and she took the lot and went home and disappeared.

What a relief! said Mummy and began to clean the floor. Now you can take it down.

Daddy took the spinster's plaster plaque off the wall and looked at it and sniffed. I looked at him and thought, now I must take mine down too. I waited to see what he was going to do. For a moment he held it over the rubbish bin. Then he went over to the bookcase and shoved the plaque behind some early statuettes of his on the top shelf. You could only just see a little bit of the glossy picture.

I climbed up onto my bunk and took my picture off the nail. I put it behind a candlestick on the bookcase and stepped backwards to have a look. It didn't look right. So I pulled the picture forward a bit, just enough so that the candlestick hid a couple of forget-me-nots. It couldn't be helped that the glossy cut-out picture was really very beautiful, and to tell the truth, for me it didn't profane anything.

The Tulle Skirt

I TURNED THE KEY AND WAITED. After a while the door opened of its own accord, very slowly as if someone inside the wardrobe was forcing it. And then the black tulle skirt poured forth and the door stood still. I did the same thing several times. Each time Mummy's tulle skirt opened out as if it was alive.

It is a party skirt which will never be used, or rather ten or a hundred transparent party skirts on top of each other, a black mountain of tulle, a great big rain cloud, or perhaps a funeral.

I crept into the wardrobe underneath the skirt and looked up inside it and now it was a lift shaft that faded away into the darkness. I pulled the hem a little. Then the tulle skirt glided out on top of me with a quiet swish. I heard the clothes hanger swing and scrape the top of the wardrobe. I sat still for a long time, I was hidden. Then I crept out of the wardrobe and the skirt came after me.

I went along the corridor inside a rain-cloud that rustled and whispered round me and felt rough against my face. No one was at home.

When I reached the studio the cloud lifted and I could see the legs of the statues and the modelling stand, but everything looked greyish-black as if there was an eclipse of the sun. Every colour was darkened and wrapped in black crepe and the studio was a new studio that I had never been in before.

I went on crawling. It was hot inside the skirt, and sometimes I couldn't see anything at all. Then I crawled in another direction and tunnels of black light opened up again and the rain was swishing the whole time.

I crawled right up to Daddy's modelling mirror which stands on the floor by the box of plaster. A great big black creature was creeping towards me.

I got cautious and stood still. The creature was shapeless. It was one of those creatures that can spread itself out and creep under the furniture or turn into a black fog that gets thicker and thicker until it is quite sticky and gets all around you and fastens itself to you.

I let the creature get a little closer and put its hand out. The hand crept along the floor and then was pulled back suddenly. The creature came even closer. Suddenly it got scared and ran quickly in an oblique direction and stopped still. Now I was scared. I kept my eyes on it the whole time. Now it was moving so slowly that you couldn't really see whether it was coming towards you or not. Occasionally its shape changed just slightly and its black tummy swept over the concrete floor. I could hardly breathe. I knew that I ought to run away and hide but I just couldn't. Now it moved diagonally again towards the wall and wasn't to be seen any longer. It was in the pile of junk behind the modelling stand, it was somewhere behind the sacks of plaster and might appear again just anywhere.

It was getting dark in the studio. I knew that it was me who had let the creature out and I couldn't capture it and lock it up again.

I crept towards the wall very slowly and began to shuffle past the bookcase. I got as far as the curtain and crawled under the work-bench. It was narrow. More and more tulle got in my face, my eyes and my mouth and the further in I crept the worse it got.

In the end I got stuck. I had wound myself into a cocoon of black tulle that smelt of powder and dust and I was completely safe. I wouldn't come out again for a whole year and when I did I would look round to see whether it was worth coming out or not. If there didn't seem to be any idea in coming out I should creep back in and stay there for the time being.

Outside in the studio the great big creature was out hunting. It multiplied itself and became many creatures. They sniffed the air and threw long shadows over the floor. Every time they called to each other they multiplied until the studio was full

of them. They rubbed up against the legs of the statues. They padded into the bedroom and jumped up on the beds so that they left deep footmarks.

Finally they all sat down in the studio window and looked out over the harbour and started to howl noiselessly.

It was then that I realised that they weren't dangerous. Of course they had heard other creatures howling at the Zoo on the island opposite the harbour. They could see the Zoo like a shadow on the other side of the ice and they were driven mad by it. An endless, melancholy prospect; a dark island full of snow and cold cages and creatures pacing up and down, up and down and howling.

I crept backwards under the work-bench and noticed that Mummy's party skirt was over my head and that it was full of bits of fluff so I shook it off and rushed around and lit the lights everywhere. I lit the lights in the studio and in the sitting-room and in the bedroom and opened lots of windows – I had so much to do – I opened the hall door and pulled back the curtain in front of the door and climbed up on the chairs and pulled out the damper of the stove and a hundred black creatures rushed past me the whole time in every direction.

There was a strong draught and the wind blew right in from the harbour through all the rooms and out on to the staircase and more and more creatures ran out until there wasn't a single one left. They laughed as they ran.

Finally it was quiet and I thought, well, well, one has to see to *everything*. But *that's* out of the way!

I put Mummy's party skirt back in the wardrobe and closed it. Then I went into the sitting-room and looked at the snowdrift. It looked very pretty in a long curve on the floor and it was getting slowly bigger. The snow whispered as it came through the window. All the creatures in the Zoo had calmed down and weren't howling any longer because now they had company. The curtains flapped in the wind and some of the drawings on the wall moved a little. The room was cold and looked quite different and I felt calm and thought that I had organised everything rather well. Actually I had only done what every decent citizen should do. I mean, *anyone* can let Danger out but the really clever thing is finding somewhere for it to go afterwards.

Snow

WHEN WE GOT TO THE STRANGE HOUSE it began to snow in quite a different way. A mass of tired old clouds opened and flung snow at us, all of a sudden and just anyhow. They weren't ordinary snowflakes, they fell straight down in large sticky lumps, they clung to each other and sank quickly and they weren't white, but grey. The whole world was as heavy as lead.

Mummy carried in the suitcases and stamped her feet on the door-mat and talked the whole time because she thought the whole thing was such fun and that everything was different.

But I said nothing because I didn't like this strange house. I stood in the window and watched the snow falling, and it was all wrong. It wasn't the same as in town. There it blows black and white over the roof or falls gently as if from heaven, and forms beautiful arches over the sitting-room window. The landscape looked dangerous too. It was bare and open and swallowed up the snow, and the trees stood in black rows that ended in nothing. At the edge of the world there was a narrow fringe of forest. Everything was wrong. It should be winter in town and summer in the country. Everything was topsy-turvy.

The house was big and empty, and there were too many rooms. Everything was very clean and you could never hear your own steps as you walked because the carpets were so big and they were as soft as fur.

If you stood in the furthest room you could see through all the other rooms and it made you feel sad; it was like a train ready to leave with its lights shining over the platform. The last room was dark like the inside of a tunnel except for a faint glow in the gold frames and the mirror which was hung too high on the wall. All the lamps were soft and misty and made a very tiny circle of light. And when you ran you made no noise.

It was just the same outside. Soft and vague and the snow went on falling and falling.

I asked why we were living in this strange house but got no proper answer. The person who cooked the food was hardly ever to be seen and didn't talk. She padded in without one noticing her and then out again. The door swung to without a sound and rocked backwards and forwards for a long time before it was still. I showed that I didn't like this house by keeping quiet. I didn't say a word.

In the afternoon the snow was even greyer and fell in flocks and stuck to the window-panes and then slid down and new flocks appeared out of the twilight and replaced them. They were like grey hands with a hundred fingers. I tried to watch one all the way as it fell, it spread out and fell, faster and faster, I stared at the next one and the next one and in the end my eyes began to hurt and I got scared.

It was hot everywhere, and there was enough room for crowds of people but there were only two of us. I said nothing.

Mummy was happy and rushed all over the place saying, what peace and quiet! Isn't it lovely and warm! And so she sat down at a big shiny table and began to draw. She took the lace tablecloth off and spread out all her illustrations and opened the bottle of Indian ink.

Then I went upstairs. The stairs creaked and groaned and made lots of noises that stairs make when a family has gone up and down them for ages. That's good. Stairs should do that sort of thing. One knows exactly which step squeaks and which one doesn't and where one has to tread if one doesn't want to make oneself heard. It was just that this staircase wasn't our staircase. Quite a different family had used it. Therefore I thought this staircase was creepy.

Upstairs all the soft lamps were on in the same way and all the rooms were warm and tidy and all the doors were standing open. Only one door

was closed. Inside it was cold and dark. It was the box-room. The other family's belongings were lying there in packing-cases and trunks and there were moth-proof bags hanging in long rows with a little snow on top of them.

Now I could hear the snow. It was falling all the time, whispering and rustling to itself and in one corner it had crept onto the floor.

The other family was everywhere in there so I shut the door and went down again and said I wanted to go to bed. Actually I didn't want to go to bed at all, but I thought it would be best. Then I wouldn't have to say anything. The bed was as wide and desolate as the landscape outside. The eider-down was like a hand too. You sank and sank right to the bottom of the earth under a big soft hand. Nothing was like it was at home, or like anywhere else.

In the morning it was still snowing in just the same way. Mummy had already got started with her work and was very cheerful. She didn't have to light fires or get meals ready and didn't have to be worried about anybody. I said nothing.

I went to the furthest room and watched the snow. I had a great responsibility and had to see what the snow was doing. It had risen since yesterday. A thousand tons of wet snow had slithered down the window-panes, and I had to climb onto a chair to see the long grey landscape. The snow had risen out there, too. The trees were thinner and more timid and the horizon had moved further away. I looked at everything until I knew that soon we would be done for. This snow had decided to go on falling until everything was a single, vast wet snow-drift, and nobody would remember what had been underneath it. All the trees would sink into the earth and all the houses. No roads and no tracks – just snow falling and falling and falling.

I went up to the box-room and listened to it falling, I heard how it stuck fast and grew. I couldn't think of anything but the snow.

Mummy went on drawing.

I was building with the cushions on the sofa and sometimes I looked at her through a peephole between them. She felt me looking and asked: are you all right? while she went on drawing. And I answered: of course. Then I crept on hands and knees into the end room and climbed onto a chair and saw how the snow was sinking down over me. Now the whole horizon had crept below the edge of the world. The fringe of forest couldn't be seen any longer, it had slid over. The world had capsized, it was turning over quietly, a little bit every day.

The very thought of it made me feel giddy. Slowly, slowly, the world was turning, heavy with snow. The trees and houses were no longer upright. They were slanting. Soon it would be difficult to walk straight. All the people on earth would have to creep. If they had forgotten to fasten their windows they would burst open. The doors would burst open. The water barrels would fall over and begin to roll over the endless field and out over the edge of the world. The whole world was full of things rolling, slithering and falling. Big things rumbled, you could hear them from far off, and you had to work out where they would come and get away from them. Here they were, rumbling past, leaping in the snow when the angle was too great, and finally falling into space. Small houses without cellars broke loose and whirled away. The snow stopped falling downwards, it flew horizontally. It fell upwards and disappeared. Everything that couldn't hold on tight rolled out into space and slowly the sky went dark and turned black. We crept under the furniture between the windows taking care not to tread on the glass. But from time to time a picture or a lamp bracket fell and smashed the window-pane. The house groaned and the plaster came loose. And outside large heavy objects rumbled past, rolling right through the whole of Finland all the way down from the Arctic Circle, and they were even heavier because they had collected so much snow as they rolled and sometimes people fell past screaming all the time.

The snow on the ground began to slither away. It slid in an enormous avalanche which grew and grew over the edge of the world ... oh no! oh no!

I rolled backwards and forwards on the carpet to make the horror of it seem greater, and in the end I saw the wall heave over me and the pictures hung straight out on their wires.

What are you doing? Mummy asked.

Then I lay still and said nothing.

Shall we have a story? she asked and went on drawing.

But I didn't want any other story than this one of my own. But one doesn't say that sort of thing. So I said: come up and look at the attic.

Mummy dried her Indian ink pen and came with me. We stood in the attic and froze for a while and Mummy said: it's lonely here, so we went back into the warmth again and she forgot to tell me a story. Then I went to bed.

Next morning the daylight was green, underwater lighting throughout the room. Mummy was asleep. I got up and opened the door and saw that the lamps were on in all the rooms although it was morning and the green light came through the snow which covered the windows all the way up. Now it had happened. The house was a single enormous snowdrift, and the surface of the ground was somewhere high up above the roof. Soon the trees would creep down into the snow until only their tops stuck out, and then the tops would disappear too and everything would level itself off and be flat. I could see it, I knew. Not even praying would stop it.

I became very solemn and quite calm and sat down on the carpet in front of the blazing fire.

Mummy woke up and came in and said: look how funny it is with snow covering the windows, because she didn't understand how serious it all was. When I had told her what had really happened she became very thoughtful.

In fact, she said after a while, we have gone into hibernation. Nobody can get in any longer and no one can get out!

I looked carefully at her and understood that we were saved. At last we were absolutely safe and protected. This menacing snow had hidden us inside in the warmth for ever and we didn't have to worry a bit about what went on there outside. I was filled with enormous relief, and I shouted, I love you I LOVE YOU, and took all the cushions and threw them at her and laughed and shouted and Mummy threw them all back and in the end we were lying on the floor just laughing.

Then we began our underground life. We walked around in our nighties and did nothing. Mummy didn't draw. We were bears with pine needles in our stomachs and anyone who dared come near our winter lair was torn to pieces. We were lavish with the wood, and threw log after log onto the fire until it roared.

Sometimes we growled. We let the dangerous world outside look after itself, it had died, it had fallen out into space. Only Mummy and I were left.

It began in the room at the end. At first it was the nasty scraping sound made by shovels. Then the snow fell down over the windows and grey light came in everywhere. Somebody tramped past outside and came to the next window and let in more light. It was awful.

The scraping sound went along the whole row of windows until the lamps were burning as if at a funeral. Outside snow was falling. The trees were standing in rows and were as black as they had been before and they let the snow fall on them and the fringe of forest on the horizon was still there.

We went and got dressed. Mummy sat down to draw.

A dark man went on shovelling outside the door and all of a sudden I started to cry and I screamed: I'll bite him! I'll go outside and bite him!

I shouldn't do that, Mummy said. He wouldn't understand. She screwed the top onto the bottle of Indian ink and said: what about going home?

Yes, I said.

So we went home.

German Measles

I HAD GERMAN MEASLES. I lay in bed in my bunk trying to crochet a kettle-holder. The eiderdown was a mountain landscape with small plaster animals wandering up and down and never getting anywhere. In the end I made an earthquake and they lay flat and didn't have to make an effort any more.

Poppolino sat in his cage on Daddy's bunk rummaging in his bits of newspaper. He lifted them up one by one and then threw them down again as if they disgusted him, stared at the ceiling and scratched his backside. His eyes looked very yellow in the wintry light.

Suddenly he was scared by his own tail which was sticking out from under the newspapers and thought it was a snake. He screamed and rushed up his tree and flung himself against the bars and shook the cage so that masses of plaster fell off the ceiling. Then he sat still looking like a miserable rat all hunched up. He pulled his long upper lip down and stared straight ahead and let his hands flop as if nothing was worth the effort. Then he fell asleep.

It was a tedious day. I turned towards the cardboard dividing-wall and looked down into the studio through my secret peephole.

Mummy was at the Mint drawing. Daddy stood in front of the modelling stand with his clay rags in his hands. He flung them onto the box of clay and swung the revolving chassis round so that it squeaked. Then he stepped backwards and looked.

He swung the chassis again and stood looking for a long while. Then he went over to the window and looked down into the street. He moved a tin and went into the sitting-room and looked out of that window. Then he went and fetched some water to water the ivy.

I turned over and tried to go to sleep but couldn't. After a while the modelling stand squeaked again. Then I heard that Daddy had gone back into the sitting-room and was rattling the loose change and nails that he had in the pockets of his overalls. He turned on the wireless and put on the headphones. Then he turned it off again and took the headphones off.

Poppolino woke up and began to scream. He shook the cage and put his face between the bars and screamed as he looked at Daddy in the sitting-room. Daddy climbed up onto his bunk and sat in front of the cage and talked very softly and I couldn't hear what he said. He opened the door and tried to put Poppolino's collar on. But Poppolino slunk away and jumped onto the sitting-room sofa and went into the studio. Then all was quiet.

Daddy climbed down again and called Poppolino. He called in his kind and treacly voice that made me very cross. Now they were both in the studio.

Poppolino was sitting on a plaster bust close to the ceiling, gaping. Daddy stood below calling him enticingly. Then it happened again.

Poppolino started swinging on the bust and then sprang. It was a big bust of an alderman and there was a frightful noise as it smashed to smithereens all over the floor. Poppolino clung to the curtains and shrieked with fright and Daddy said nothing. Then something just as big crashed to the floor, but I only heard the noise as I daren't look any longer.

When all was quiet again I assumed that Poppolino had taken refuge on Daddy's shoulder and was being consoled. In a while they would go out for a walk in the park. I listened carefully. The Daddy put on Poppolino's velvet jacket and hat. Daddy talked the whole time he was doing up the buttons and the hat ribbon and Poppolino was saying how rotten and beastly everything was. Now they were out in the hall. The door made a clicking noise as they went out.

I got out of bed and took all my plaster animals and threw them down into the sittingroom. I

climbed down the steps and fetched the hammer and bashed them to powder and rubbed the plaster into the carpet with my feet. Then I climbed up and crept into Poppolino's cage. I sat in his bits of newspaper and breathed German measles on everything as hard as I could.

When they came home again I could tell that they had been to the shop and bought liquorice and herrings. I lay under the bedclothes and heard Daddy put Poppolino back into his cage. He talked away in a cheerful voice and I took it that Poppolino had been given some liquorice. Then Daddy came over to my bunk and tried to give me some liquorice too.

Monkey food! I said. I don't want to eat the same things as someone who smashes statues.

But it wasn't a good one, Daddy said. It was good that Poppolino knocked it over. How do you feel now?

I shall soon be dead, I answered, and crept lower down the bed.

Don't be silly, Daddy said. When I didn't answer he went into the studio and started working. He was whistling. I heard him walking up and down in front of the modelling stand, whistling and working.

I felt my guilty conscience in my toes, and before it could creep any higher I sat up quickly and started to crochet. I wasn't going to make a kettle-holder any longer. It would be a pullover for Poppolino.

It's difficult to tell why or how people cheer up and get the feeling they want to work. It's not easy to be sure about germs either. Best not to think about it too much but try and put everything right as quickly as possible with a good deed.

Flying

I DREAMED THAT THOUSANDS OF PEOPLE were running in the street. They weren't shouting but you could hear the sound of their boots on the pavement, many thousands of boots, and there was a red glow in the studio from outside. After a while there weren't so many of them running and in the end there were only the steps of the last one, who was running in such a way that he fell over and then picked himself up and ran on.

Then everything started shrinking. Every piece of furniture became elongated and narrow and disappeared towards the ceiling. There was something crawling under the rag rugs in the hall. It was also narrow and thin and wriggled in the middle, sometimes very quickly and sometimes very slowly.

I tried to get into the bedroom where Mummy had lit the oil lamp but the door was shut. Then I ran up the steps to the bunk. The door of Poppolino's cage was open and I could hear him padding round somewhere in the dark and whining, which is something he always does when it is very cold or when he feels lonely.

Now it came up the steps, grey and limping. One of its legs had come off. It was the ghost of the dead crow. I flew into the sitting-room and bumped about on the ceiling like a fly. I could see the sitting-room and the studio underneath me in a deep well that sank deeper and deeper.

I thought more about that dream afterwards, particularly about the flying part, and decided to fly as often as possible.

But it didn't work and I dreamed about all the wrong things, and in the end I made up my own dreams myself just before I went to sleep or just after I had woken up. I started by thinking up the most awful things I could, which wasn't particularly difficult. When I had made things as awful as possible I took a run and bounced off the floor and flew away from everything, leaving it all behind me in a deep well. Down there the whole town was burning. Down there Poppolino was padding around in the studio in the dark screaming with loneliness. Down there sat the crow saying: it was your fault that I died. And the Unmentionable Thing crawled under the mat.

But I just went on flying. In the beginning I bumped about on the ceiling like a fly, but then I ventured out of the window. Straight across the street was the farthest I could fly. But if I glided I could go on as long as I wanted, right down to the bottom of the well. There I took another leap and flew up again.

It wasn't long before they caught sight of me. At first they just stopped and stared, then they started to shout and point and came running from all directions. But before they could reach me I had taken another leap and was up in the air again laughing and waving at them. They tried to jump after me. They ran to fetch step-ladders and fishing-rods but nothing helped. There they were, left behind below me, longing to be able to fly. Then they went slowly home and got on with their work.

Sometimes they had too much work to do and sometimes they just couldn't work which was horrid for them. I felt sorry for them and made it possible for them all to fly.

Next morning they all woke up with no idea of what had happened and sat up and said: another miserable day begins! They climbed down from their bunks and drank some warm milk and had to eat the skin too. Then they put on their coats and hats and went downstairs and off to their work, dragging their legs and wondering whether they should take the tram. But then they decided to walk in any case because one is allowed to take a tram for seven stops but not really for five, and in any case fresh air is healthy.

One of them came down Wharf Road and a lot of wet snow stuck to her boots. So she stamped a little to get rid of the snow – and sure enough, she flew into the air! Only about six feet, and then came down again and stood wondering what had happened to her. Then she noticed a gentleman running to catch the tram. It rang its bell and was off so he ran even faster and the next moment he was flying too. He took off from the ground and described an arc in the air up to the roof of the tram and there he sat!

Then Mummy began to laugh as hard as she could and immediately understood what had happened and cried ha! ha! ha! and flew onto Victor Ek's roof in a single beautiful curve. There she caught sight of Daddy in the studio window rattling nails and coins in the pockets of his overall and she shouted: jump out! Come flying with me!

But Daddy daren't until Mummy flew over and sat on the window-sill. Then he opened the window and took hold of her hand and flew out and said: well I'll be damned!

By that time the whole of Helsinki was full of amazed people flying. No one did any work. Windows were open all over the place and down in the street the trams and the cars were empty and it stopped snowing and the sun came out.

All the new-born babies were flying and all the very old people and their cats and dogs and guinea-pigs and monkeys – just everybody!

Even the President was out flying!

The roofs were crowded with picnickers undoing their sandwiches and opening bottles and shouting cheers! to one another across the street and everyone was doing precisely what he or she wanted to do.

I stood in the bedroom window watching the whole thing and enjoying myself no end and wondering how long I should let them go on flying. And I thought that if I now made everything normal again it might be dangerous. Imagine what would happen if the following morning they all opened their windows and jumped out! Therefore I decided that they could be allowed to go on flying until the end of the world in Helsinki.

Then I opened my bedroom window and climbed onto the window-ledge together with the crow and Poppolino. Don't be afraid! I said. And so off we flew.

Christmas

THE SMALLER YOU ARE, the bigger Christmas is. Underneath the Christmas Tree, Christmas is vast. It is a green jungle with red apples and sad, peaceful angels twirling around on cotton thread keeping watch over the entrance to the primaeval forest. In the glass balls the primaeval forest is never-ending; Christmas is a time when you feel absolutely safe, thanks to the Christmas tree.

There outside is the studio which is very big and very cold. The only warm place is close to the stove, with the fire and the shadows on the floor and the pillar-like legs of the statues.

The studio is full of sculpture, large white women who have always been there. They are everywhere, the movements of their arms are vague and shy and they look straight past one because they are uninterested, and sad in quite a different way from my angels. Some of them have clay rags on their heads and the largest one has a clothesline round her tummy. The rags are wet and when one goes past they brush one's face like cold white birds in the dark. It's always dark in the evening.

The studio window must never be cleaned because it gives a very beautiful light, it has a hundred little panes, some of them darker than others, and the lanterns outside swing to and fro and draw a window of their own on the wall. There are stout shelves, one under the other, and on each shelf white ladies stand, but they are quite tiny. They face one another and turn away from one another but their movements are just as hesitant and shy as those of the big women. All of them get dusted just before Christmas. But only Mummy is allowed to touch them and the grenades from the 1918 war aren't dusted at all.

Daddy's women are sacred. He doesn't care about them after they are cast in plaster, but for everybody else they are sacred.

Apart from the women, the window and the stove, everything else is in shadow. Against the wall there is a sinister heap of things that mustn't be examined; armatures, boxes with clay and plaster, moulds, wood, rags and modelling stands, and behind them all creeps the mysterious thing with eyes as black as night.

But the middle of the room is empty. All there is is a single modelling stand with a woman in wet rags, and she is the most sacred thing of all. The stand has three legs and they throw stiff shadows across the blank patch of concrete floor and up towards the ceiling which is so far away that no one can get up there, at least not before the Christmas tree arrives. We have the finest and tallest tree in the town and it's probably worth a fortune because it has to reach right up to the ceiling and be of the bristly kind. All other sculptors have small and scruffy Christmas trees, not to mention certain painters who hardly have what you could call trees at all. People who live in ordinary flats have their tree on a table with a *cloth* on it, poor things! They buy their tree as an afterthought.

On the morning agreed upon beforehand we, that is Daddy and I, get up at six o'clock because Christmas trees must be bought in the dark. We walk from Skatudden to the other end of town because the big harbour there is just the right setting for buying a Christmas tree. We generally spend hours choosing, looking at every branch very suspiciously, because they can be stuck in. It's always cold. Once Daddy got the top of a tree in his eye. The early morning darkness is full of freezing bundles hunting for trees and the snow is scattered with fir twigs. There is a menacing enchantment about the harbour and the market place.

Then the studio is transformed into a primaeval forest where one can make oneself unget-at-able deep in under the Christmas tree. Under the tree

one must feel full of love. There are also other places where one can feel full of grief or hate, between the hall doors where the letters drop through the letter-box, for example. The hall door has small red and green glass panes, it is narrow and solemn, and the hall is full of clothes, skis and packing cases, but it is between the two doors that there is just enough room to stand and hate. If one hates in a big space one dies immediately. But if the space is narrow the hate turns inwards again and goes round and round one's body and never reaches God.

But it's quite different with Christmas trees, particularly when the glass balls have been hung up. They are store-places for love and that's why it's so terribly dangerous to drop them.

As soon as the Christmas tree was in the studio everything took on a fresh significance, and was charged with a holiness that had nothing to do with Art. Christmas began in earnest.

Mummy and I went to the icy rocks behind the Russian Church and scratched around for some moss. We built the Land of the Nativity with the desert and Bethlehem in clay, with new streets and houses each time, we filled the whole of the studio window, we made lakes with pieces of mirror and placed the shepherds and gave them new lambs and new legs because the old ones had broken up in the moss and we placed the sand carefully so that the clay could be used later. Then we took out the manger with the thatched roof which they had got in Paris in nineteen hundred and ten. Daddy was very moved and had to have a snorter.

Mary was always right in the front, but Joseph had to be at the back with the cattle because he had been damaged by water and, besides, in perspective he was smaller.

Last of all came the Baby Jesus, who was made of wax and had real curly hair which they had made in Paris before I was born. When he was in place we had to be quite quiet for a long while.

Once Poppolino got out and devoured the Baby Jesus. He climbed up Daddy's Statue of Liberty, sat on the hilt of the sword, and ate up Jesus.

There was nothing we could do, and we didn't dare to look at each other. Mummy made a new Baby Jesus of clay and painted it. We thought that it turned out too red and too fat round the middle, but no one said anything.

Christmas always rustled. It rustled every time, mysteriously, with silver paper and gold paper and tissue paper and a rich abundance of shiny paper decorating and hiding everything and giving a feeling of reckless extravagance.

There were stars and rosettes everywhere, even on the vegetable dishes and on the expensive shop-bought sausages which we used to have before we began to have real ham.

One could wake up at night to the reassuring sound of Mummy wrapping up presents. One night she painted the tiles of the stove with little blue landscapes and bunches of flowers on every tile all the way to the top.

She made gingerbread biscuits shaped like goats with the pastry-cutter and gave the Lucy-pussies, small flat pastry scrolls, curly legs and a raisin in the middle of the tummy. When they came here from Sweden the pussies had only four legs but every year they got more and more until they had a wild and curly ornamentation all over.

Mummy weighed sweets and nuts on a letter-balance so that everyone would get exactly the same amount. During the year everything is measured roughly, but at Christmas everything has to be absolutely fair. That's why it's such a strenuous time.

In Sweden people stuff their own sausages and make candles and carry small baskets to the poor for several months and all mothers sew presents at night. On Christmas Eve they all become Lucias, with a great wreath with lots of candles in it on their heads.

The first time Daddy saw a Lucia he was very scared, but when he realised it was only Mummy he began to laugh. Then he wanted her to be a Lucia every Christmas Eve because it was such fun.

I lay on my bunk and heard Lucia starting to climb the steps, and it wasn't easy for her. The whole thing was as beautiful as being in heaven and she had modelled a pig in marzipan as they do in Sweden. Then she sang a little and climbed up the steps to Daddy's bunk. Mummy only sings once a year because her vocal cords are crossed.

There were hundreds of candles on the balustrade round our bunks waiting to be lit just before the Story of the Nativity. Then they flutter in all directions round the studio like so many pearl necklaces, maybe there are thousands of them. These candles are very interesting when they burn down because the cardboard dividing-wall could easily catch fire.

Later in the morning Daddy used to get very worked up because he took Christmas very seriously and could hardly stand all the preparations. He was quite exhausted. He put every single candle straight and warned us about the danger of fire. He rushed out and bought mistletoe, a tiny twig of it, because it had to hang from the ceiling and is more expensive than orchids. He kept on asking whether we were quite sure that everything was in order and suddenly thought that the composition of the Land of the Nativity was all wrong. Then he had a snorter to calm himself. Mummy wrote poetry and picked sealing-wax off wrapping-paper and gold ribbon from the previous Christmas.

Twilight came and Daddy went to the churchyard with nuts for the squirrels and to look at the graves. He has never been particularly concerned about the relations lying there and they didn't particularly like him either because they were distant relatives and rather bourgeois. But when Daddy got back home again he was sad and twice as worked up because the churchyard had been so wonderfully beautiful with all the candles burning there. Anyway, the squirrels had buried masses of nuts along with the relatives although it was forbidden to do so, and that was a consoling thought at least.

After dinner there was a long pause to allow Christmas a breathing-space. We lay on our bunks in the dark listening to Mummy rustling down by the stove and in the street outside all was quiet.

Then the long lines of candles were lit and Daddy leaped down from his bunk to make sure that the ones on the Christmas tree were all upright and that the candle behind Joseph wasn't setting fire to the thatched roof.

And then we had the Story of the Nativity. The most solemn part was when Mary pondered these things in her heart and it was almost as beautiful when they departed into their own country another way. The rest of it wasn't so special.

We recovered from this and Daddy had a snorter. And now I was triumphantly certain that Christmas belonged to me.

I crept into the green primaeval forest and pulled out parcels. Now the feeling of love under the branches of the tree was almost unbearable, a compact feeling of holiness made up of Marys and angels and mothers and Lucias and statues, all of them blessing me and forgiving everything during the year that was past, including that business of hating in the hall, forgiving everything on earth as long as they could be sure that everybody loved one another.

And just then the largest glass ball fell on the concrete floor and it smashed into the world's tiniest and nastiest splinters.

The silence afterwards was unbelievable. At the neck of the ball there was a little ring with two metal prongs. And Mummy said: actually, that ball has always been the wrong colour.

And so night came and all the candles had burnt down and all the fires had been put out and all the ribbons and paper had been folded up for next Christmas. I took my presents to bed with me.

Every now and then Daddy's slippers shuffled down there in the studio and he ate a little pickled herring and had a snorter and tried to get some music out of the wireless he had built himself. The feeling of peace everywhere was complete.

Once something happened to the wireless and it played a whole tune before the interference came back. In its own way interference is something of a miracle, mystifying isolated signals from somewhere out in space.

Daddy sat in the darkened studio for a long time eating pickled herring and trying to get proper tunes on the wireless. When it didn't work at all he climbed up on to his bunk again and rustled his newspapers. Mummy's candles had gone out much earlier, and there was a general smell of Christmas tree and burning and benediction all over.

Nothing is as peaceful as when Christmas is over, when one has been forgiven for everything and one can be normal again.

After a while we packed the holy things away in the hall cupboard and the branches of the Christmas tree burnt in the stove with small violent explosions. But the trunk wasn't burnt until the following Christmas. All the year it stood next to the box of plaster, reminding us of Christmas and the absolute safety in everything.

A note on the photos

All images © Jansson Family archive

Inside covers:
Front: Tove Jansson as a child
Back: Tove's parents, Viktor Jansson and Signe
        Hammarsten ('Ham'), in early married life

Also by Tove Jansson, published by Sort Of

THE SUMMER BOOK

'The Summer Book is a marvellously uplifting read, full of gentle humour and wisdom.' Justine Picardie, *Daily Telegraph*

An elderly artist and her six-year-old grand-daughter while away a summer together on a tiny island in the Gulf of Finland. As the two learn to adjust to each other's fears, whims and yearnings, a fierce yet understated love emerges – one that encompasses not only the summer inhabitants but the very island itself.

Written in a clear, unsentimental style, full of brusque humour, *The Summer Book* is a profoundly life-affirming story. Tove Jansson captured much of her own life and spirit in the book, which was her favourite of her adult novels. This edition has a foreword by Esther Freud.

A WINTER BOOK

'As smooth and odd and beautiful as sea-worn driftwood, as full of light and air as the Nordic summer. We are lucky to have these stories collected at last.' Philip Pullman

A Winter Book features thirteen stories from Tove Jansson's first book for adults, *Sculptor's Daughter* (1968), along with seven of her most cherished later stories (from 1971 to 1996). Drawn from youth and age, this selection by Ali Smith provides a thrilling showcase of the great Finnish writer's prose, scattered with insights and home truths. It includes afterwords by Philip Pullman, Esther Freud and Frank Cottrell Boyce.

FAIR PLAY

'So what can happen when Tove Jansson turns her attention to her own favourite subjects, love and work, in the form of this novel about two women, lifelong partners and friends? Expect something philosophically calm – and discreetly radical. At first sight it looks autobiographical. Like everything Jansson wrote, it's much more than it seems … *Fair Play* is very fine art.' From Ali Smith's introduction.

What mattered most to Tove Jansson, she explained in her eighties, was work and love, a sentiment she echoes in this tender and original novel. *Fair Play* portrays a love between two older women, a writer and an artist, as they work side by side in their Helsinki studios, travel together and share summers on a remote island. In the generosity and respect they show each other and the many small shifts they make to accommodate each other's creativity we are shown a relationship both heartening and truly progressive.

THE TRUE DECEIVER

'I loved this book. It's cool in both senses of the word, understated yet exciting … the characters still haunt me.' Ruth Rendell

In the deep winter snows of a Swedish hamlet, a strange young woman fakes a break-in at the house of an elderly artist in order to persuade her that she needs companionship. But what does she hope to gain by doing this? And who ultimately is deceiving whom? In this portrayal of two women encircling each other with truth and lies, nothing can be taken for granted. By the time the snow thaws, both their lives will have changed irrevocably.

TRAVELLING LIGHT

'Jansson's prose is wondrous: it is clean, deliberate; an aesthetic so certain of itself it's breathtaking.' Kirsty Gunn, *Daily Telegraph*

Travelling Light takes us into new Tove Jansson territory. A professor arrives in a beautiful Spanish village only to find that her host has left and she must cope with fractious neighbours alone; a holiday on a Finnish Island is thrown into disarray by an oddly intrusive child; an artist returns from abroad to discover that her past has been eerily usurped. With the deceptively light prose that is her hallmark, Tove Jansson reveals to us the precariousness of a journey – the unease we feel at being placed outside of our milieu, the restlessness and shadows that intrude upon a summer.

ART IN NATURE

An elderly caretaker at a large outdoor exhibition, called Art in Nature, finds that a couple have lingered on to bicker about the value of a picture; he has a surprising suggestion that will resolve both their row and his own ambivalence about the art market. A draughtsman's obsession with drawing locomotives provides a dark twist to a love story. A cartoonist takes over the work of a colleague who has suffered a nervous breakdown, only to discover that his own sanity is in danger. In these witty, sharp, often disquieting stories, Tove Jansson reveals the faultlines in our relationship with art, both as artists and as consumers. Obsession, ambition, and the discouragement of critics are all brought into focus in these wise and cautionary tales.

Tove Jansson

The Finnish-Swedish writer and artist TOVE JANSSON
(1914–2001) is best known as the creator of the Moomin
stories, which were first published in English sixty years
ago and have remained in print ever since. However, in
her fifties she turned her attention to writing for adults,
producing four novels and eight story collections.

Sculptor's Daughter, published in Swedish in 1968, was
her first book for adults – a sequence of stories based on
her memories of a Helskinki childhood. It was followed
by a story collection, *The Listener* (1971), and her novel,
The Summer Book (1973), a Scandinavian classic, and a
bestseller when reissued in English by Sort Of Books.

Sort Of Books have also published translations of Tove
Jansson's novel *The True Deceiver* and the story collections
Travelling Light, Fair Play, Art in Nature (originally *The Doll's
House*), and an anthology, *The Winter Book*. In 2013 Sort
Of Books published an English edition of the 'forgotten'
first ever Moomin book, *The Moomins and the Great Flood*,
originally published in 1945.

Author photo © Beata Bergström

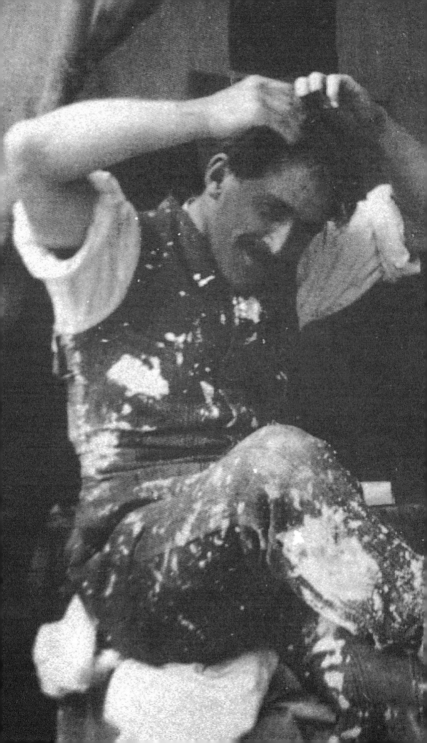